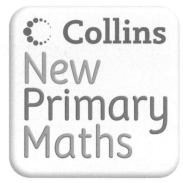

Collins New Primary Maths

Pupil Book 5C

Series Editor: Peter Clarke

Authors: Jeanette Mumford, Sandra Roberts, Andrew Edmondson

Contents

Numbers in the hundred thousands

● **Explain what a digit represents in whole numbers and partition, round and order these numbers**

 1 Put each set of numbers in order smallest to largest.

a
85 353
62 354
84 287
92 351
35 627

b
28 365
28 148
28 654
28 307
28 749

c 17 268
71 395
17 215
17 521
71 591

d Choose one number from each set and write it out in words.

2 Write the value of the red digit.

a 68 354
b 38 214
c 72 351
d 82 155

e 30 024
f 14 625
g 72 391
h 61 320

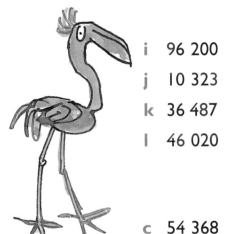

i 96 200
j 10 323
k 36 487
l 46 020

3 Write the next ten numbers that came after these.

a 30 562
d 15 266

b 41 210
e 63 788

c 54 368
f 42 307

 1 Put each set of numbers in order smallest to largest.

a

325 200   954 641   427 325   684 296   157 364

b

598 327   571 304   534 963   532 594   504 112

c

342 269   343 648   334 562   324 957   334 957

d Choose one number from each set and write it out in words.

2 Write the value of the red digit.

a 542 698	**b** 364 287	**c** 210 954
d 308 559	**e** 746 921	**f** 436 952
g 749 300	**h** 869 230	**i** 694 297

3 Round each of the numbers in question **2** to the nearest 100 000.

4 Write the next ten numbers that came after these.

a 483 058	**b** 674 294	**c** 239 184
d 856 921	**e** 470 365	**f** 561 596

Reach the target

Work in twos, threes or fours.

1 Write one of these numbers at the top of your paper. Each player must choose a different number.

285 635   285 641   285 653   285 658

The target number is 285 700.

2 Next to the number write the number that comes next. Then give your paper to the player sitting next to you.

3 Write the next number. Give your paper to the next player.

4 Keep going until somebody writes 285 700. They are the winner.

You need:
- a sheet of paper each
- a pencil each

Variation

Play again with these numbers.

547 109

547 115

547 123

547 127

The target number is 547 150.

Ordering decimals

 ① Copy out the number lines and put the decimal numbers in the correct place on them.

a 4·6   4·8   4·7   4·2

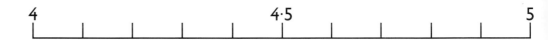

4   4·5   5

b 8·8   8·1   8·3   8·9

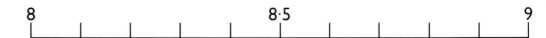

8   8·5   9

c 2·6   2·9   2·2   2·4

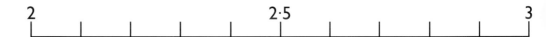

2   2·5   3

d 6·7   6·3   6·1   6·8

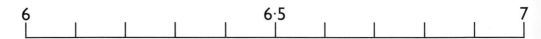

6   6·5   7

② Round each decimal number in question ① to the nearest whole number.
Use their place on the number line to help you.

① Put these parcels in order of weight, lightest to heaviest.

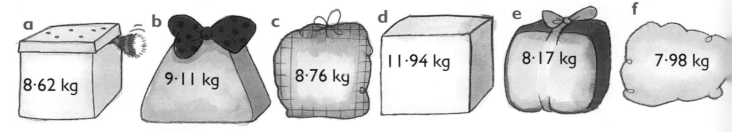

a 8·62 kg   **b** 9·11 kg   **c** 8·76 kg   **d** 11·94 kg   **e** 8·17 kg   **f** 7·98 kg

Put these t-shirts in order of how far they have run, shortest to longest distance.

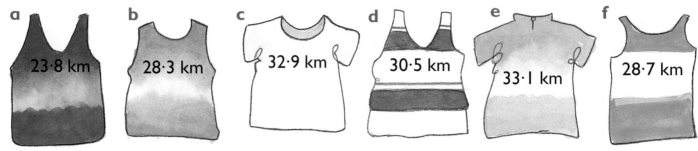

a 23·8 km   b 28·3 km   c 32·9 km   d 30·5 km   e 33·1 km   f 28·7 km

3 Put these containers in order of how much they hold, smallest to largest.

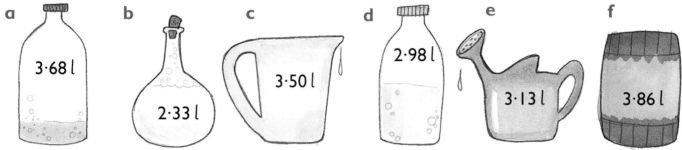

a 3·68 l   b 2·33 l   c 3·50 l   d 2·98 l   e 3·13 l   f 3·86 l

4 Put these children in order of how long they held their breath for – longest time to shortest time.

a 8·21 s   b 8·38 s   c 9·22 s   d 8·76 s   e 9·46 s

5 Round all the quantities in questions **1**, **2**, **3** and **4** to the nearest whole number.

Example

8·62 kg rounds up to 9 kg

These sets of numbers are a mixture of one- and two-place decimals. Order each set.

a 14·31   14·4   14·8   14·76   14·01
b 26·5   26·52.   26·87   26·9   26·2

c 178·01   178·1   178·12   178·26   178·6
d 86·99   86·09   86·9   86·19   86·1

e 362·5   362·05   362·4   362·14   362·1
f 54·3   54·13   54·03   54·31   54·1

Decimal sums and differences

Write each decimal and the other decimal that goes with it to total 10.

Example

4·3

4·3 + 5·7 = 10

HINT

Use your knowledge of pairs of numbers that total 10.

a 2·4 10 ?

b 6·7 10 ?

c 8·1 10 ?

d 9·6 10 ?

e 7·6 10 ?

f 1·8 10 ?

g 7·5 10 ?

h 3·2 10 ?

i 4·9 10 ?

j 5·3 10 ?

k 8·6 10 ?

l 3·5 10 ?

1 Copy and complete.

a 3·56 + 2·71

b 1·14 + 4·37

c 0·71 + 5·06

d 4·66 + 6·83

e 3·59 + 7·99

f 8·15 + 6·77

g 2·19 + 5·47

h 6·31 + 4·36

i 4·02 + 7·59

j 7·40 + 8·82

2 Explain how you worked out these calculations.

3 Choose 3 addition calculations from question **1**. Write out the two-digit calculation that is similar.

4 Work out the answers to these subtractions by finding the difference between the two numbers. Show your working out.

a 5·87 – 3·43

b 3·57 – 1·83

c 9·36 – 5·71

d 8·03 – 7·68

e 4·21 – 2·85

f 6·81 – 4·55

g 9·99 – 3·72

h 4·27 – 0·69

i 7·22 – 1·62

j 7·84 – 6·53

Look at these calculations. Think of two different methods for working out the answer to each one.

Explain clearly which method you prefer for the addition and which method you prefer for the subtraction and why.

8·67 + 7·84

7·12 – 3·68

Checking calculations

 1 Round these numbers to the nearest 10.

a 87   b 23   c 11   d 18   e 72

2 Round these numbers to the nearest 100.

a 203   b 396   c 187   d 509   e 93

3 Round these numbers to the nearest 1000.

a 1992   b 3020   c 2106   d 4851   e 962

4 Work out each calculation using your calculator.
Repeat the calculation to check your answer.

a 27×16 b $450 - 279$ c $586 \div 8$
d $821 + 598$ e 69×11 f $3306 \div 58$

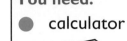

You need:
● calculator

1 Work out each calculation using your calculator.

a 59×11 b $607 - 395$ c 21×38

d $489 \div 992$ e $288 \div 9$ f 22×71

g $608 \div 19$ h $1207 - 592$ i $1805 \div 95$

You need:
● calculator

2 Check your answers to question **1**.
Work out an approximate calculation.
Show your working.

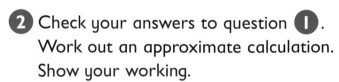

Example

Calculator: $31 \times 19 = 589$
Approximate calculation: $30 \times 20 = 600$
The two answers are close, so the
calculator answer is probably correct.

3 Work out each calculation using
your calculator.

a $258 + 673$ b 93×48 c $2007 \div 9$

d $972 - 359$ e $1944 \div 54$ f 112×17

g $5329 - 1842$ h 88×88 i $9000 - 4621$

4 Check your answers to
question **3**.
Work backwards.
Show your working.

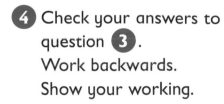

Example

Calculator $1368 \div 57 = 24$
Work backwards $24 \times 57 = 1368$
The answer is correct.

● Use your calculator to answer these questions.
Check each answer using the most efficient method.

a How long are 23 skipping
ropes joined together?

1·83 m

b How much more expensive
is the blue bicycle?

£60.21   £38.77

c How much drink does each person get?

 Jungle
juice
4320 ml

d How far is Thurso from Exeter?

371 miles   352 miles

Thurso   Carlisle   Exeter

e The cost of 11 cakes is £16.28.
How much does one cake cost?

f There are 250 envelopes in a box.
How many in 17 boxes?

 1 Work out each calculation using your calculator.

a 19 × 9 − 61
b 493 + 712 − 385
c 936 ÷ 18 + 108
d 21 × 31 − 405

e 2142 + 6060 − 3951
f 29 × 39 × 9
g 3504 ÷ 48 − 29
h 103 × 62 + 986

You need:
● calculator

2 Check your answers to question **1**.
Work out an approximate calculation.

3 Use your calculator to answer these questions.
Check each answer using the most
efficient method.

Example

Calculator   38 × 96 − 982 = 2666
Approximate   40 × 100 − 1000
calculation   = 4000 − 1000 = 3000
Fairly close, so calculator answer is
probably correct.

a Calculate the total cost.

£8125   £6999   £9852

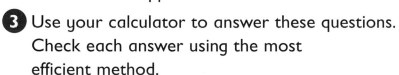
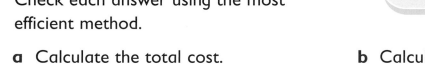

b Calculate the cost of nine bottles of
shampoo and a sponge.

£1.82

£3.10

11

Shopping problems

Solve one- and two-step problems involving whole numbers and decimals, choosing and using appropriate calculation strategies

1 Harriet goes into the fruit shop. Work out the price of each of the items that she buys. Show all your working out.

a She buys a banana, pays with a £1 coin and gets 55p change.

b She buys a pineapple, pays with a £1 coin and gets 13p change.

c She buys an avocado, pays with a £2 coin and gets 72p change.

d She buys a melon, pays with a £2 coin and gets 33p change.

e She buys an apple, pays with a £2 coin and gets £1.81 change.

f She buys some grapes, pays with a £2 coin and gets 57p change.

g She buys a punnet of strawberries, pays with a £2 coin and gets 4p change.

h She buys a bag of lemons, pays with a £2 coin and gets £1.32 change.

2 Use your answers to work out how much it would cost if Harriet bought three of each fruit.

1 Harry goes into the stationery shop. Work out the price of one of each of the items that he buys. Show all your working out.

a He buys 3 pens, pays with a £2 coin and receives £1.25 change.

b He buys 4 notepads, pays with a £2 coin and receives 20p change.

c He buys 2 books, pays with a £5 note and receives £2.30 change.

d He buys 3 bookmarks, pays with a £5 note and receives £3.86 change.

e He buys 6 pencils, pays with a £2 coin and receives 62p change.

f He buys 7 pencil cases, pays with a £10 note and receives 90p change.

2 This problem has been worked out but a mistake has been made. Look at the working out and work out where the mistake is. Copy the working out into your book and then change it so it is right.

Hilary goes into the newsagents and buys 5 packets of stickers and a comic. The comic cost £1.75. She paid with a £5 note and got 65p change.

What is the price of one packet of stickers?

£5.00 − 65p = £4.35

£4.35 − £1.75 = £2.50

£2.50 ÷ 5 = 50p

What would you say to the person who did this working out so they wouldn't make the same mistake again?

Using the prices from question ❶ in the ⬤ section, work out how much Harry would have had to pay each time if the shop reduced everything by 25%.
If the prices are not exact, the shop always rounds up.

Multiplication and division facts

● Know by heart multiplication and division facts

A multiplication square

×	2	3	4	5	6	7	8	9	10
2	4	6	8	10	12	14	16	18	20
3	6	9	12	15	18	21	24	27	30
4	8	12	16	20	24	28	32	36	40
5	10	15	20	25	30	35	40	45	50
6	12	18	24	30	36	42	48	54	60
7	14	21	28	35	42	49	56	63	70
8	16	24	32	40	48	56	64	72	80
9	18	27	36	45	54	63	72	81	90
10	20	30	40	50	60	70	80	90	100

1 You should know these multiplication facts by heart, but you can check the answers on the multiplication square if you need to.

a 9×6 3×7 4×8 8×8

b 4×6 7×9 6×8 7×7

c 9×8 3×9 4×7 6×9

2 Find all of the multiplication facts that equal these numbers.

(12) (18) (24) (40) (54)

 1 Write down the number on the blank pin.

a
90
360

Example
4 × 90 = 360

b
70
420

c
40
200

d
80
5600

e
90
810

f
400
2400

g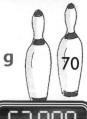
70
63 000

Knock any pins over and the numbers are multiplied together!

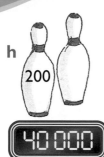 h 200

 i 400

 j 6

 k 9000

 40 000

 72 000

3600

540 000

> The scoreboards show your total score after each throw.

2 If you knock over two pins each time, write which pins could have been knocked over.

a  480

b 1200

c 24 000

d 7200

e 5400

f  100 000

g 8000

h 30 000

i 4200

j 12 000

Times it!

Instructions

For 2 to 3 players

1 Draw up a score sheet with the players' names at the top. Give each player a starting number of 500.

2 Take turns to roll the two dice. Multiply the numbers together.

3 Subtract the answer from the start number to give a new total. Keep a running score.

4 The first person to reach 0 is the winner.

You need:

- 2 × 1–12 dice
- a pencil
- a scoresheet

A	B
500	500

More multiplication methods

 Choose five calculations. Approximate the answer first then use the grid method to work out the answer.

Example

23×18 ○○○ $20 \times 20 = 400$

×	20	3	
10	200	30	230
8	160	24	+ 184
			414
			1

a 16×27

b 33×22

c 563×8

d 629×7

e $6 \cdot 3 \times 8$

f $9 \cdot 7 \times 6$

g 29×29

h 834×6

i $8 \cdot 8 \times 4$

1 Multiply each of the numbers in the box by the number on top of the box. Approximate your answers first.

a
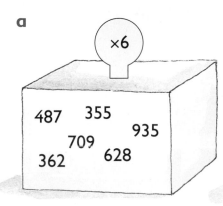
×6

487 355 935 709 628 362

b
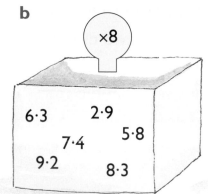
×8

6·3 2·9 5·8 7·4 9·2 8·3

2 Approximate your answer first.
Use the standard method of recording to work out the answer to each calculation.

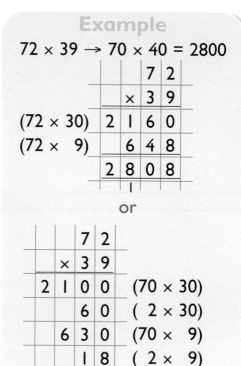

Example

72 × 39 → 70 × 40 = 2800

```
              7  2
          ×   3  9
(72 × 30) 2 1 6  0
(72 ×  9)   6 4  8
          2 8 0  8
              1
```

or

```
          7 2
       ×  3 9
       2 1 0 0   (70 × 30)
           6 0   ( 2 × 30)
         6 3 0   (70 ×  9)
           1 8   ( 2 ×  9)
       2 8 0 8
           1
```

a   22 × 34

b   21 × 47

c   31 × 38

d   32 × 63

e   42 × 28

f   55 × 39

g   33 × 27

h   24 × 56

i   52 × 94

j   35 × 74

Remember
Keep the numbers
in the correct
columns!

1

Use each of these four digits once.
Arrange them to make a **product** as
close as possible to 1000.

or

2

Use each of these four digits once.
Arrange them to make a **product** as
close as possible to 5000.

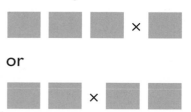

or

Division methods

Write multiplication facts for each bag.

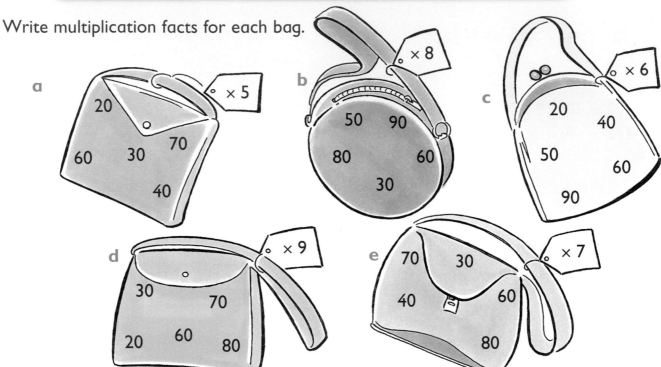

a
20
70
60 30
40
× 5

b
50 90
80 60
30
× 8

c
20
40
50
60
90
× 6

d
30
70
20 60 80
× 9

e
70 30
40 60
80
× 7

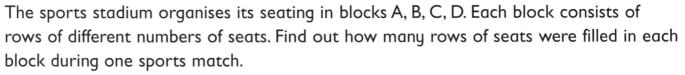

The sports stadium organises its seating in blocks A, B, C, D. Each block consists of rows of different numbers of seats. Find out how many rows of seats were filled in each block during one sports match.

Copy the tables. Approximate your answer first.

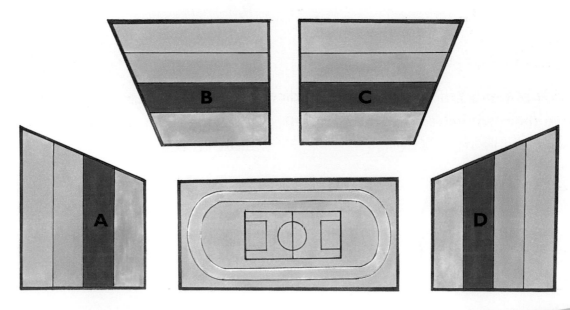

Record your working using a standard written method of division.

 6 seats per row

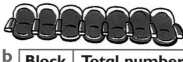 7 seats per row

a
Block	Total number of seats	Total number of rows
A	336	
B	384	
C	282	
D	474	

b
Block	Total number of seats	Total number of rows
A	406	
B	483	
C	357	
D	574	

 8 seats per row 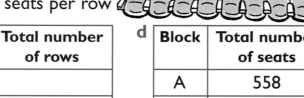 9 seats per row

c
Block	Total number of seats	Total number of rows
A	424	
B	472	
C	360	
D	592	

d
Block	Total number of seats	Total number of rows
A	558	
B	657	
C	522	
D	774	

Divide it!

A game for 2 players

1 Roll the 4 dice.

2 Make the smallest three-digit number you can and write this down.

3 Divide the number on the remaining dice into the three-digit number. Show your working.

4 Check your answer with your partner's work.

(If you throw one or two zeros work the answer out mentally or use jottings.)

You need:
● four 0–9 dice
● paper and pencil

Example

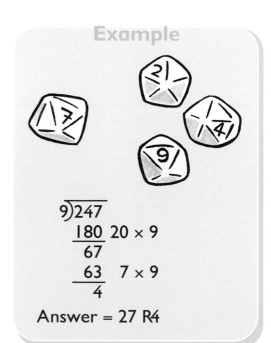

$$9\overline{)247}$$
$$\underline{180} \quad 20 \times 9$$
$$67$$
$$\underline{63} \quad 7 \times 9$$
$$4$$

Answer = 27 R4

More division methods

Use efficient written methods to divide HTU ÷ U

Approximate the answer to each calculation. The first one is done for you.

a
Example

$346 ÷ 6 \rightarrow 60$ $(360 ÷ 6 = 60)$

b $248 ÷ 5$ g $456 ÷ 6$ l $378 ÷ 9$

c $332 ÷ 4$ h $362 ÷ 8$ m $467 ÷ 7$

d $496 ÷ 5$ i $576 ÷ 8$ n $283 ÷ 9$

e $256 ÷ 3$ j $389 ÷ 6$ o $627 ÷ 9$

f $275 ÷ 3$ k $156 ÷ 4$ p $562 ÷ 4$

Approximate your answer first.
Choose a standard written method of recording to work out the answer to each calculation.

Example

$686 ÷ 8 \rightarrow$ $(640 ÷ 8 = 80)$

$$8\overline{)686}$$
$$\underline{640} \quad (80 × 8)$$
$$46$$
$$\underline{40} \quad (5 × 8)$$
$$6$$

Answer = 85 R6

or

$686 ÷ 8 \rightarrow$ $(640 ÷ 8 = 80)$

$$\begin{array}{r} 85 \ \text{R6} \\ 8\overline{)686} \\ \underline{64} \\ 46 \\ \underline{40} \\ 6 \end{array}$$

a $386 ÷ 7$

c $863 ÷ 9$

b $269 ÷ 5$

d $452 ÷ 6$

e $285 ÷ 3$

Remember

Keep the numbers in the correct columns!

f 498 ÷ 8

g 627 ÷ 7

h 376 ÷ 7

i 207 ÷ 8

j 398 ÷ 9

1 Five answers equal 55. Can you find them?

a 495 ÷ 9

b 270 ÷ 6

c 360 ÷ 8

d 275 ÷ 5

e 385 ÷ 7

f 330 ÷ 6

g 455 ÷ 7

h 175 ÷ 5

i 440 ÷ 8

j 585 ÷ 9

2 Five answers equal 79. Can you find them?

a 356 ÷ 4

b 474 ÷ 6

c 316 ÷ 4

d 712 ÷ 8

e 632 ÷ 8

f 801 ÷ 9

g 623 ÷ 7

h 553 ÷ 7

i 711 ÷ 9

j 534 ÷ 6

Solving word problems

● **Choose and use appropriate operations to solve word problems**

For each word problem, decide which operation you will use to answer the question.

a French fries cost [ ] . Jim buys [ ] . How much does he spend?

b It costs [ ] for [ ] burgers. How much do they cost?

c Samuel buys a hot dog, a can of drink and an ice-cream. How much does he spend?

d A carton of drink cans costs [ ] . Each can costs [ ] . How many cans in a carton?

e Mrs Joseph has [ ] . She pays [ ] for her food. How much change does she get?

f Hot dogs cost [ ] each. How much does it cost for [ ] ?

Read the word problems. Choose an appropriate method of calculating your answer.
● mental
● mental with jottings
● paper and pencil

Show all your working.

a Oak Tree School has 486 pupils. Nine coaches were hired to take them to the sports stadium. How many children were there on each coach?

b The school prepared packed lunches. Each packed lunch was put into a carton holding 19 lunches. 18 cartons were required. How many packed lunches were made?

c Each child at Oak Tree School contributed £2 towards the cost of the coaches. How much money was collected?

d From each class, 21 children entered the 100 m sprint races. There are 14 classes in Oak Tree School. How many children ran a sprint race?

e Oak Tree School sat in Stand A. There are 525 seats in Stand A. Each row has seven seats. How many rows of seats altogether?

f 12 schools competed in the relay races. Each team had four runners. How many children were there altogether in the relays?

Use the pictures and information on both pages to write your own word problems for these calculations.

a £4.86 × 4   **b** £5.25 − £4.86   **c** 14p × 12
d £4.86 ÷ 6   **e** £14.32 + £12.87   **f** 278 ÷ 9

Written addition

- Use efficient written methods to add whole numbers and decimals

 Work out the answers to these calculations. Be sure to make an estimate first.

1
a 482 + 234

b 345 + 527

c 227 + 354

d 652 + 274

e 437 + 246

f 728 + 237

g 259 + 690

h 407 + 239

i 565 + 305

j 724 + 138

Example

563 + 264

Estimate: 800

```
    5 6 3
+   2 6 4
    8 2 7
    1
```

Remember to estimate the answer first.

Don't forget to line up the decimal points.

2
a £16.72 + £20.26

b £15.81 + £42.07

c £24.21 + £35.65

d £34.28 + £25.31

e £48.61 + £50.37

Example

£16.72 + £20.26

Estimate: £37

```
    £16.72
+   £20.26
    £36.98
```

3
a 5·83 m + 3·14 m

b 6·42 kg + 2·39 kg

c 9·72 cm + 2·06 cm

d 4·89 m + 5·05 m

e 5·72 km + 3·75 km

Write these calculations out vertically, make an estimate and then work out the answers. Be sure to write the digits in the correct columns.

1 a 6832 + 149   g 5125 + 907

 b 4136 + 793   h 6254 + 389

 c 5872 + 516   i 8834 + 207

 d 4341 + 467   j 4468 + 645

 e 5107 + 738   k 8045 + 579

 f 3263 + 654   l 9324 + 858

2 a £26.84 + £13.52

 b £17.62 + £21.52

 c £53.41 + £37.24

 d £52.12 + £29.38

 e £37.86 + £15.61

 f £49.72 + £23.18

3 a 4·32 m + 5·75 m

 b 5·82 cm + 2·40 cm

 c 6·72 kg + 6·19 kg

 d 6·72 km + 2·59 km

 e 8·65 km + 5·27 km

 f 7·95 m + 2·62 m

1 Look at all the calculations in the ⬤ activity. Investigate the pattern of adding odd and even numbers. How could you use this pattern to check your results?

Odd + odd = ?
Odd + even = ?
Even + even = ?

2 What happens if more than two numbers are added?

Adding more than 2 numbers

● **Use efficient written methods to add whole numbers**

Write these calculations out vertically, make an estimate and then work out the answers. The first one is done for you.

a   2638 + 1125

Example

Estimate: 3700

```
a   2 6 3 8
  + 1 1 2 5
    3 7 6 3
      1
```

Remember

Write the digits in the right columns!

b   3672 + 1135

c   2067 + 3492

d   3721 + 2554

e   2162 + 3753

f   3047 + 8532

g   4215 + 9206

h   3263 + 4819

i   4127 + 8391

j   5621 + 2639

Write these calculations out vertically, make an estimate and then work out the answers. The first one is done for you.

a   4662 + 2104 + 1415

b   3748 + 6052 + 2131

c   2462 + 1670 + 2543

d   5036 + 6427 + 7205

e   2451 + 7260 + 3191

f   4683 + 2832 + 1950

g   6804 + 3832 + 4941

h   7284 + 1357 + 1263

i   4623 + 1738 + 2206

j   8921 + 5302 + 9745

k   7062 + 9242 + 9341

l   8219 + 5254 + 6123

Example

Estimate: 8000

```
a   4 6 6 2
    2 1 0 4
  + 1 4 1 5
    8 1 8 1
      1   1
```

Remember

Write the digits in the right columns!

 ## Add them up

Play this game in twos
or threes.

1 Take turns to roll the dice
four times and make a four-
digit number.

2 Each player writes down the
two (if two players) or three
(if three players) numbers
and adds them together.

3 After everyone has finished
adding, use a calculator to
check the answers.

4 The first player to get the
correct answer scores 1
point. The winner is the first
player to collect 5 points.

You need:

● a 1-6 dice

● paper and
pencil each

● calculator

Written subtraction

● **Use efficient written methods to subtract whole numbers and decimals**

Work out the answers to these calculations.
Be sure to make an estimate first.

1
a 947 – 319
b 862 – 435
c 725 – 362
d 605 – 241
e 513 – 272
f 468 – 129
g 806 – 534
h 937 – 308
i 572 – 237
j 824 – 458

Example

864 – 583
Estimate: 300

$$\begin{array}{r} {}^{7}{}^{\,1}\!86\!4 \\ - \;\,583 \\ \hline 281 \end{array}$$

2
a £16.28 – £12.13
b £21.47 – £19.35
c £37.83 – £26.71
d £29.45 – £18.38
e £45.37 – £31.62

3
a 8·72 km – 3·21 km
b 6·86 m – 2·72 m
c 7·15 kg – 3·58 kg
d 9·62 m – 5·18 m
e 8·12 km – 3·40 km

Write these calculations out vertically, make an estimate and then work out the answers. Be sure to write the digits in the correct columns.

1
a 5862 – 235
b 7435 – 908
c 4920 – 751
d 6137 – 408
e 8492 – 378
f 5024 – 617

g 8154 – 827
h 9264 – 539
i 6748 – 689
j 8246 – 528
k 7594 – 835
l 4761 – 872

2
a £46·12 – £37·08
b £37·41 – £28·27
c £47·26 – £19·07
d £54·35 – £27·51
e £65·74 – £31·85
f £91·58 – £39·09

3
a 8·94 m – 3·27 m
b 12·73 cm – 8·55 cm
c 15·04 kg – 7·32 kg
d 9·27 km – 6·82 km
e 17·83 km – 9·26 km
f 18·63 m – 9·07 m

Change these measures to the same unit and then subtract them.
a 8·25 km – 750 m
b 7·47 kg – 483 g
c 6·51 m – 189 cm
d 15·73 km – 847 m
e 24·67 kg – 627 g

Adding and subtracting in your head

● **Use knowledge of place value and addition and subtraction of two-digit numbers to derive sums and differences**

1 Work out the calculations in your head.
Use the answer to the first calculation to help you work out the second.

a 28 + ☐ = 100   328 + ☐ = 400   f 29 + ☐ = 100   529 + ☐ = 600
b 52 + ☐ = 100   452 + ☐ = 500   g 38 + ☐ = 100   438 + ☐ = 500
c 34 + ☐ = 100   734 + ☐ = 800   h 55 + ☐ = 100   655 + ☐ = 700
d 81 + ☐ = 100   681 + ☐ = 700   i 42 + ☐ = 100   742 + ☐ = 800
e 67 + ☐ = 100   267 + ☐ = 300   j 73 + ☐ = 100   873 + ☐ = 900

2 Work out what goes with the decimal to equal the next whole number.
Use the answer to the first calculation to help you work out the second.

a 0·8 + ☐ = 1   2·8 + ☐ = 3   e 0·3 + ☐ = 1   5·3 + ☐ = 6
b 0·4 + ☐ = 1   2·4 + ☐ = 3   f 0·7 + ☐ = 1   1·7 + ☐ = 2
c 0·2 + ☐ = 1   3·2 + ☐ = 4   g 0·6 + ☐ = 1   5·6 + ☐ = 6
d 0·1 + ☐ = 1   4·1 + ☐ = 5   h 0·5 + ☐ = 1   7·5 + ☐ = 8

3 Add and subtract these pairs of decimals.

a 2·3 + 1·4 = ☐   f 5·6 − 2·3 = ☐
b 1·5 + 1·2 = ☐   g 4·8 − 3·5 = ☐
c 2·6 + 2·1 = ☐   h 4·6 − 1·3 = ☐
d 3·3 + 3·5 = ☐   i 5·9 − 4·1 = ☐
e 3·7 + 2·1 = ☐   j 6·8 − 2·7 = ☐

Work out the calculations in your head.

1 a 428 + ☐ = 500   f 435 + ☐ = 600
b 651 + ☐ = 700   g 751 + ☐ = 800
c 168 + ☐ = 200   h 816 + ☐ = 900
d 546 + ☐ = 600   i 529 + ☐ = 600
e 873 + ☐ = 900   j 982 + ☐ = 1000

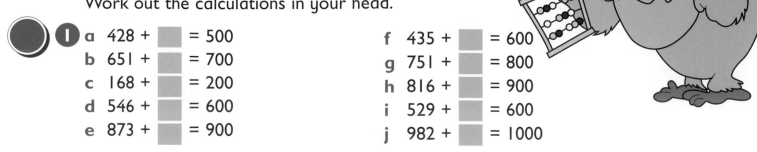

2 a 4·8 + ☐ = 5
   b 3·7 + ☐ = 4
   c 8·1 + ☐ = 9
   d 4·6 + ☐ = 5
   e 5·7 + ☐ = 6

   f 3·2 + ☐ = 4
   g 9·3 + ☐ = 10
   h 1·5 + ☐ = 2
   i 7·9 + ☐ = 8
   j 8·4 + ☐ = 9

3 a 5·7 + 2·5 = ☐
   b 4·6 + 3·8 = ☐
   c 2·7 + 3·9 = ☐
   d 3·5 + 5·6 = ☐
   e 4·2 + 6·8 = ☐

   f 8·3 + 1·9 = ☐
   g 7·8 + 2·4 = ☐
   h 6·5 + 7·7 = ☐
   i 3·6 + 4·6 = ☐
   j 7·1 + 5·9 = ☐

4 a 6·2 – 3·8 = ☐
   b 4·5 – 2·7 = ☐
   c 3·4 – 2·7 = ☐
   d 6·8 – 5·9 = ☐
   e 7·4 – 3·8 = ☐

   f 6·1 – 3·5 = ☐
   g 6·2 – 2·7 = ☐
   h 9·2 – 5·4 = ☐
   i 8·1 – 3·6 = ☐
   j 7·2 – 5·4 = ☐

5 a 0·26 + 0·54 = ☐
   b 0·85 + 0·47 = ☐
   c 0·61 + 0·39 = ☐
   d 0·78 + 0·51 = ☐
   e 0·33 + 0·84 = ☐

   f 0·47 + 0·69 = ☐
   g 0·99 + 0·21 = ☐
   h 0·61 + 0·37 = ☐
   i 0·48 + 0·73 = ☐
   j 0·86 + 0·49 = ☐

6 Now choose one calculation from each ⬤ activity and explain how you worked it out.

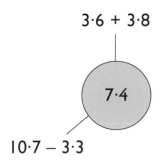

Write 7·4 in the middle of your page. Think of as many addition and subtraction calculations where the answer is 7·4. Make them as different as possible.

3·6 + 3·8

7·4

10·7 – 3·3

Money raising

Every time a school sells one of its hats, it gets 60p for the school fund.

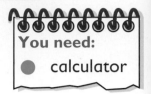
You need:
● calculator

a One family buys 5 hats. How much does the school fund get?

b In one week 9 hats are sold. How much money goes to the school fund?

c If the school fund gets £3.60, how many hats were sold?

d If the school fund gets £7.80, how many hats were sold?

e One week 3 hats were sold and the following week 5 hats were sold. How much money did the school make in these two weeks?

Solve these problems using a calculator. You must show your working out.
A charity sells its badges in lots of shops. Every time one is sold, the charity gets 65p.

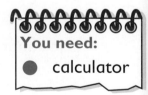
You need:
● calculator

a One shop made £4.55 one week for the charity. How many badges did they sell?

b Another shop made £7.15 in a week. How many badges did they sell?

c How much did the charity make that week from these two shops?

d If one shop sells 4 badges and another shop sells 8 badges, how much does the charity get?

e In a different week, the charity made £18.20 altogether. One shop had sold 9 badges. How many badges had the other shop sold?

f The charity has set itself a target of making £20 a week during May. What is the minimum number of badges they need to sell in a week?

A charity sells its badges in lots of shops. Every time one is sold, the charity gets 65p.

A generous well-wisher tells the charity that they would like to help them by donating another 25p for every badge that is sold on one given day. The charity found that the total number of badges sold on that day totals 134.

a How much did the charity make from the sales?

b How much will the well-wisher need to give them?

c What will be the total amount they make?

You need:
● calculator

Rounding remainders

● **Round up or down after division, depending on the context**

Work out the answers to these calculations. Be careful – some have remainders!

a	26 ÷ 4 =	g	45 ÷ 6 =	m	61 ÷ 9 =
b	38 ÷ 5 =	h	38 ÷ 7 =	n	48 ÷ 8 =
c	27 ÷ 3 =	i	24 ÷ 6 =	o	29 ÷ 9 =
d	42 ÷ 5 =	j	54 ÷ 6 =	p	37 ÷ 9 =
e	18 ÷ 2 =	k	47 ÷ 7 =	q	64 ÷ 8 =
f	25 ÷ 3 =	l	56 ÷ 7 =	r	43 ÷ 8 =

Read each word problem. Write the division calculation and answer. If there is a remainder, think carefully whether you need to round your answer up or down.

a In one day 186 people went on the dodgem cars. Each dodgem car holds two people. How many times were the dodgem cars used?

b The rollercoaster seats four people per carriage. There are 298 people in the queue. How many carriages are required?

c Joshua has saved £58 to spend on rides. All rides cost £3. How many rides can he go on?

d The Fairy Floss stall made £125 in one day. Bags of Fairy Floss cost £2. How many bags were sold?

e Doughnuts are sold in packs of six. One batch of mixture makes 374 doughnuts. How many packs can be made up?

f The Youth Group has raised £467 for the day trip to the theme park. Entrance fees cost £9 per person. How many people can go?

g In one day 676 people went on the ghost train. Each carriage holds eight people. How many carriages were filled?

Write your own word problems that involve rounding the answer up or down.

The arrow ⬆ means to round the answer up.

The arrow ⬇ means to round the answer down.

Choose five of the calculations below.

327 ÷ 5 ⬆

48 ÷ 9 ⬇

124 ÷ 7 ⬆

63 ÷ 10 ⬆

264 ÷ 8 ⬇

55 ÷ 6 ⬇

74 ÷ 9 ⬆

163 ÷ 7 ⬇

Fraction remainders

● **Express a quotient as a fraction when dividing whole numbers**

 Work out the answers to these calculations. Write any remainders as a fraction.

a	$14 \div 3 =$	h	$19 \div 2 =$	o	$91 \div 9 =$
b	$32 \div 6 =$	i	$39 \div 6 =$	p	$54 \div 5 =$
c	$84 \div 9 =$	j	$37 \div 4 =$	q	$69 \div 6 =$
d	$21 \div 7 =$	k	$50 \div 8 =$	r	$32 \div 3 =$
e	$29 \div 4 =$	l	$32 \div 3 =$	s	$80 \div 8 =$
f	$43 \div 5 =$	m	$52 \div 6 =$	t	$66 \div 6 =$
g	$61 \div 10 =$	n	$72 \div 8 =$	u	$22 \div 4 =$

Read each word problem.
Write a division calculation for each problem.
Record any remainders as a fraction.

a There are four children per group. Each group is given 13 chocolate cupcakes to share evenly between them. How many cakes do they get each?

b There are 74 chocolate biscuits to share between four groups. How many chocolate biscuits are there per group?

c There are 17 chocolate eclairs. Only five children like them. How many eclairs does each child receive?

d There are 25 packets of choco-beans to share equally between 10 children. How many packets does each child receive?

e The class teacher put aside 15 doughnuts to share with the staff for morning tea. There are 10 staff altogether. How many doughnuts per teacher?

f There are 47 choco-beans in each tube. Two children share each tube. How many choco-beans per child?

g There are 39 chocolate bars to share between four groups. How many chocolate bars per group?

h There are 5 children per group and 67 sweets per group. How many sweets are there per child?

Hit the target

Use each set of cards shown. Make division calculations.
How close can you get to the target number?
Write your answers as a fraction.
Put a star beside the calculation that gives the answer closest to the target.

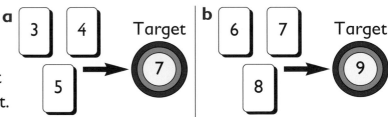

Example

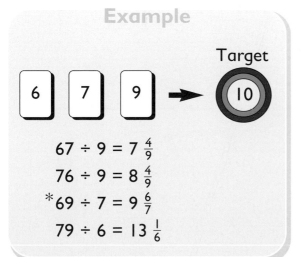

Target

6 7 9 → 10

$67 \div 9 = 7\frac{4}{9}$
$76 \div 9 = 8\frac{4}{9}$
$*69 \div 7 = 9\frac{6}{7}$
$79 \div 6 = 13\frac{1}{6}$

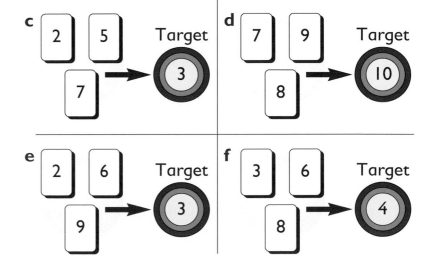

Money and decimals

Divide these amounts of pounds by the numbers given.
Give your answers in pence.

a   £1 ÷ 4 =

b   £1 ÷ 2 =

c   £1 ÷ 10 =

d   £1 ÷ 5 =

e   £2 ÷ 4 =

f   £3 ÷ 5 =

g   £2 ÷ 10 =

h   £4 ÷ 5 =

i   £3 ÷ 4 =

j   £5 ÷ 10 =

k   £3 ÷ 10 =

l   £2 ÷ 5 =

Work out the answer to each word problem.
Show all your workings.

Acorn School has 10 classes.
They raised money to spend on
books and games for each class.

a   Acorn School spent £474 on
dice and spinners for each class.
How much was spent per class?

b   The two Year 5 classes were given
£155 to spend on dictionaries.
How much is this per class?

c   The headteacher allocated £695 between
the 10 classes to be spent on games. How
much did each class receive?

d The four infant classes spent £194 on picture books for their reading corners. How much was spent by each class?

e The school purchased 10 hardback books for the library. How much was each book if the total cost was £81?

f The school asked local businesses to donate money to the school. Five businesses donated £236 between them. If each business donated the same amount, how much did they each donate?

Win or lose?

Instructions

A game for 2 to 4 players.

1 Shuffle the cards and place them face down in the centre of the table.

2 Take turns to select a card.

3 Take the required amount of money from the bank.

4 Roll the dice. Divide your money by the number on the dice using notes or coins from the bank to help you.

5 Check with the other players to see if you are correct.

You need:

- money (notes and coins)
- blank dice with the numbers 2, 2, 4, 4, 5, 10
- 10 cards with these amounts written twice: £1, £2, £3, £4, £5

Multiplication and division lucky dip

Look at each of the following calculations. Some of the answers are incorrect.
Rewrite each of the incorrect calculations with the correct answer.

a
$4 \times 600 = 2400$

b
$260 \times 2 = 520$

c
$86 \times 5 = 411$

d
$6000 \div 100 = 6$

e
$83 \times 3 = 219$

f
$500 \div 2 = 200$

g
$8000 \div 100 = 8$

h
$72 \times 4 = 148$

i
$370 \times 2 = 74$

j
$7 \times 300 = 1000$

k
$65 \times 3 = 130$

l
$420 \div 2 = 210$

m
$70 \times 5 = 35$

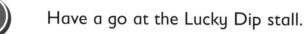

Have a go at the Lucky Dip stall.
Choose calculations from the Lucky Dips. Then work out the answers.
Your teacher will tell you how many lucky dips to choose.

a

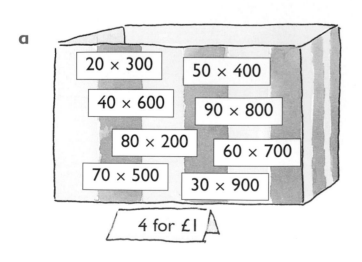

20×300	50×400
40×600	90×800
80×200	60×700
70×500	30×900

4 for £1

b

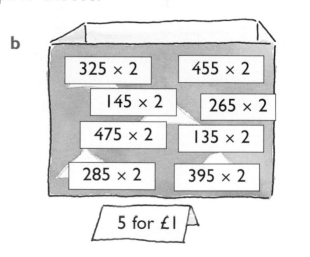

325×2	455×2
145×2	265×2
475×2	135×2
285×2	395×2

5 for £1

c
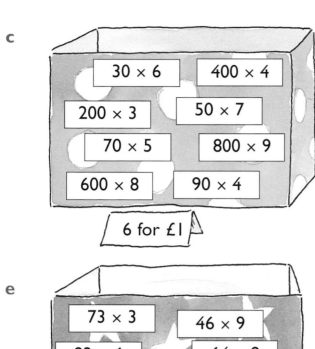

30 × 6   400 × 4

200 × 3   50 × 7

70 × 5   800 × 9

600 × 8   90 × 4

6 for £1

d
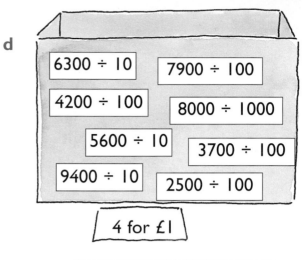

6300 ÷ 10   7900 ÷ 100

4200 ÷ 100   8000 ÷ 1000

5600 ÷ 10   3700 ÷ 100

9400 ÷ 10   2500 ÷ 100

4 for £1

e
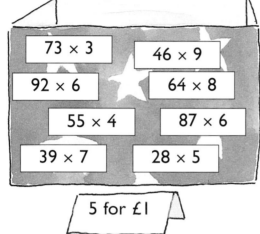

73 × 3   46 × 9

92 × 6   64 × 8

55 × 4   87 × 6

39 × 7   28 × 5

5 for £1

f
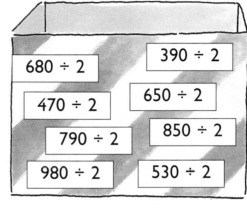

390 ÷ 2

680 ÷ 2   650 ÷ 2

470 ÷ 2

790 ÷ 2   850 ÷ 2

980 ÷ 2   530 ÷ 2

6 for £1

Three children played a place value game.
They recorded their work on a place value chart.
They wrote down their starter number and then turned
over operation cards and recorded the answers until they
reached their final score.
Find out who had the highest score.
Record your work on a place value chart.

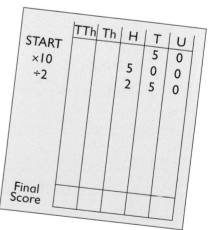

	TTh	Th	H	T	U
START ×10 ÷2			5 2	5 0 5	0 0 0
Final Score					

	Start									
Child 1	50	×10	÷2	÷2	×10	×2	÷100	×7	×2	×100
Child 2	26	×6	×2	×10	÷2	÷2	÷2	÷10	×7	×100
Child 3	75	×9	×2	×10	÷100	×2	×2	×100	÷10	×2

Doubling and halving

Some numbers can be made easier to calculate with by doubling or halving.
Find the numbers below that are easy to multiply by.
Write whether you would double or halve the number to help you
with a mental calculation.

14

31

23

18

17

Example

$14 \rightarrow \frac{1}{2}$ of $14 = 7$

50

27

25

20

13

16

22

5

12

You know these doubling and halving strategies already.

To × 50
First
× 100
then halve

To × 16
First × 8
then double

To × 8
First × 4
then double

To × 5
First × 10
then halve

To × 20
First × 10
then double

It is easy to multiply by 12, 14 and 18 also.
Turn each number on page 43 into a number that is a known fact by halving.
When you get the answer, double it to get your final answer.

Example

$15 \times 14 \rightarrow$ Turn 14 into 7 by halving
$15 \times 7 = 105$
Double your answer: $105 \times 2 = 210$
So $15 \times 14 = 210$

Choose one number from each side. Multiply the two numbers together. Use a doubling or halving strategy to help you work out the answers.

Your teacher will tell you how many calculations to make.

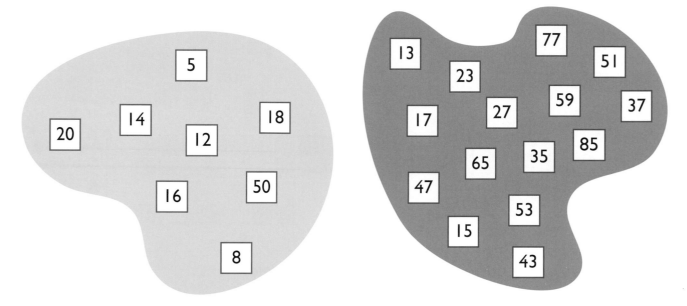

Easy multiplying (It's like noughts and crosses)

Instructions

A game for 2 players.

1 Choose two numbers from the labels on the left. Multiply them together using doubling or halving to help.

2 If your answer is on the grid, put a counter on that square.

3 The winner is the first person to get three in a row.

You need:

● 6 counters each (one colour per player)

14	34	19
50	63	18
47	25	16

850	2350	288
1197	893	450
224	3150	476

Rectangle research

 1 Arrange the 36 squares to make a rectangle.

2 Count how many squares make up the length and how many squares make up the width.

3 Record your results in a table.

width in squares	length in squares
4	9

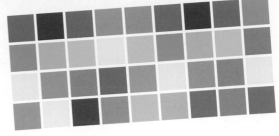

4

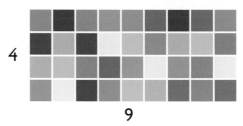

9

You need:
● 36 squares

4 Use the same 36 squares to make different rectangles. Find as many as you can.

Record your results in the table.

 1 Statement: *With 12 squares you can make 3 different rectangles.*

True or false?
Draw each different rectangle on squared paper.
Record your results in a table.

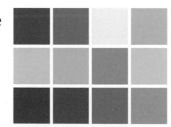

You need:
● a supply of squares or cubes
● 1 cm squared paper

2 a Statement: *24 squares can be arranged to make exactly 4 different rectangles.*

Investigate.
Draw each different rectangle on squared paper. Record your results in a table.

length in squares	width in squares
6	4

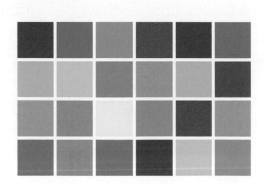

b What if you had 48 squares?

Can you make exactly 6 different rectangles?
Do not draw the rectangles.
List their dimensions in a table.

3 Count all the squares in this diagram
Work in a systematic way.
Begin with the smallest size of square.

 1 Count all the rectangles in this diagram.
Work in a systematic way.
Begin with the smallest rectangle.
Use the diagrams below to help you.

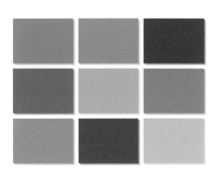

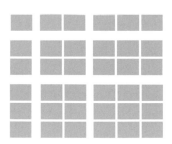

2 Copy and complete this table for
the rectangles you find.

3 Write about the patterns
you notice.

		length in units		
		1	2	3
width in units	1			
	2			
	3			
	total			

Puzzling pentominoes

Investigate a general statement about familiar shapes by finding examples that satisfy it

 ① Using the pentominoes in the ⬤ activity, write the letter of the pentomino that will complete these rectangles.

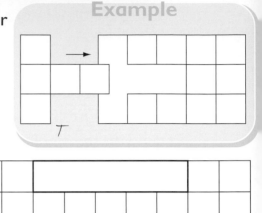

Example

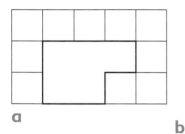

a

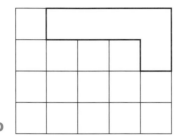

b

c

② a Fit together the pentominoes S and W to make this shape.

b Find two different pentominoes to make the reflection.

c Draw both shapes and label the pentominoes you used.

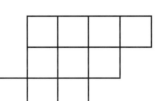

You need:
- ⬤ I cm squared paper
- ⬤ ruler

 A pentomino is a shape made from five identical squares touching edge to edge. They can look like some of the letters of the alphabet.

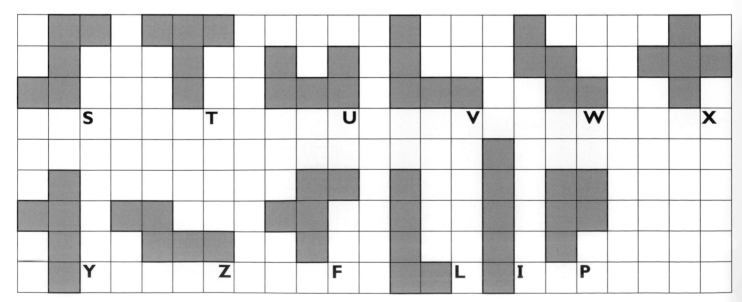

For each question, copy the shape on to squared paper and use two colours to show the different pentominoes.

Example

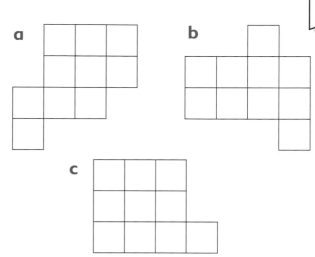

P + Z   U + X

You need:
● I cm squared paper
● ruler
● coloured pencils

Divide each shape into two pentominoes.

a Find two different ways for shape **a**.

b Find three different ways for shape **b**.

c Find four different ways for shape **c**.

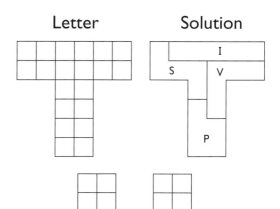

This double-size T has 20 squares.
It is made with a set of four pentominoes.

1 Make this double-size U using the pentominoes L, S, V and Z.
Record on squared paper. Use colour to identify each pentomino.

2 Using four different pentominoes each time, make these double-size letters. Record them on squared paper. Colour the individual pentominoes in each shape.

Letter   Solution

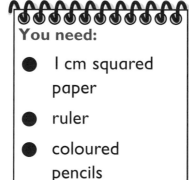

You need:
● I cm squared paper
● ruler
● coloured pencils

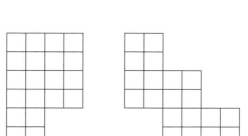

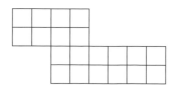

Check the net

These shapes are nets for six 1-6 dot dice.

● Copy each net on to 1 cm squared paper.
● Fill in the missing dots so that opposite faces add up to 7.

You need:

● 1 cm squared paper

● ruler

a

b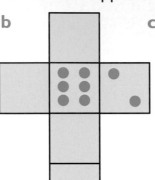

c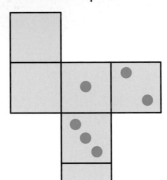

d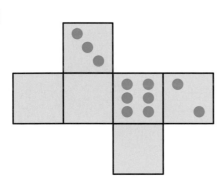

e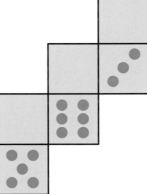

f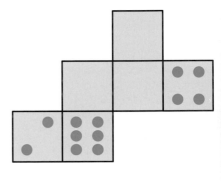

1 Some of the shapes on page 49 are nets of closed cubes.
Make each shape with your interlocking
square tiles, then fold it up.

You need:

● 6 interlocking square tiles

2 Copy and complete this table.
Enter ✓ if the shape is a net of a cube.
Enter ✗ if the shape is not.

shape	Is a net of a cube
a	✓
b	
c	

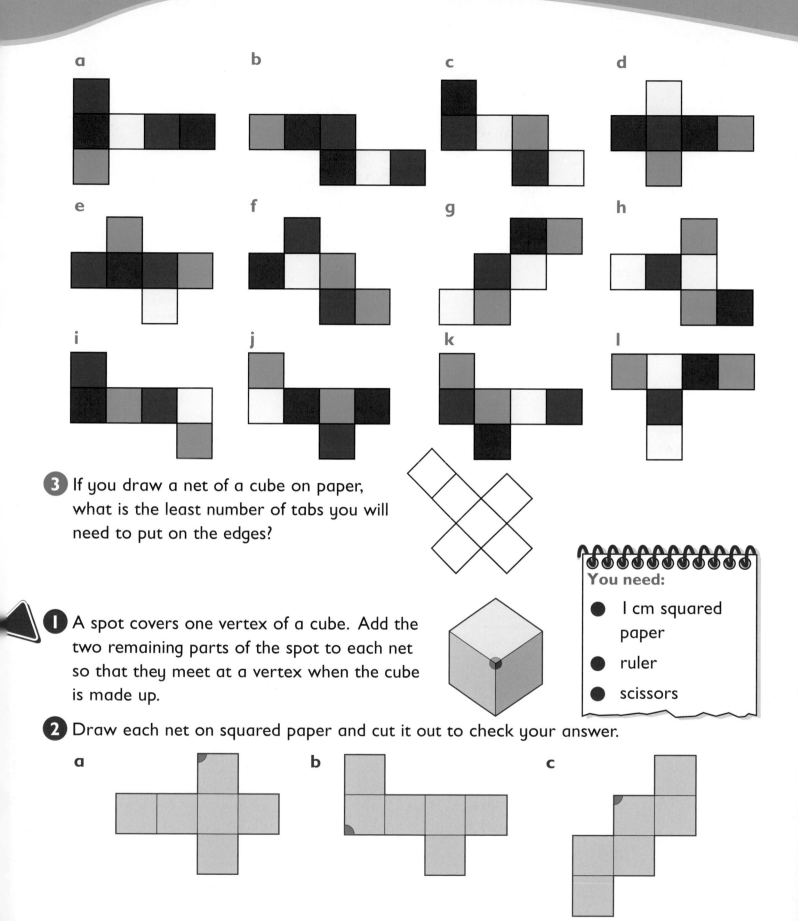

a   b   c   d

e   f   g   h

i   j   k   l

3 If you draw a net of a cube on paper, what is the least number of tabs you will need to put on the edges?

You need:
- 1 cm squared paper
- ruler
- scissors

1 A spot covers one vertex of a cube. Add the two remaining parts of the spot to each net so that they meet at a vertex when the cube is made up.

2 Draw each net on squared paper and cut it out to check your answer.

a   b   c

49

Angles in parallelograms, kites and regular shapes

 1 For each regular polygon, measure all its angles.

2 Match the polygon to the size of its interior angle.

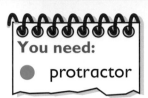 **You need:**
● protractor

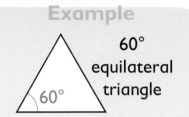 **Example**
60° equilateral triangle
60°

90°

120°

144°

108°

135°

128°

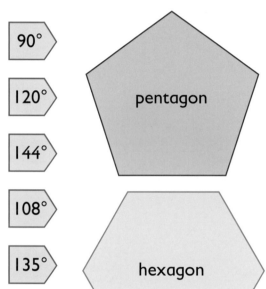 pentagon

heptagon

decagon

 hexagon

square

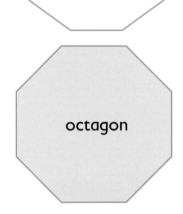 octagon

 1 Copy parallelograms 1, 2 and 3 on to 1 cm square dot paper.

 **You need:**
● 1 cm square dot paper
● protractor ● ruler

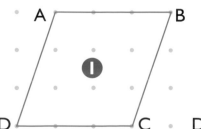
A   B

D   C

1

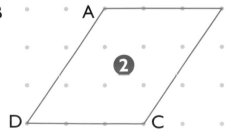
A   B

D   C

2

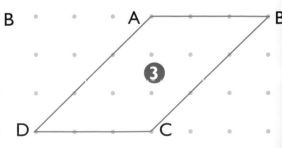
A   B

D   C

3

2 Draw the next two parallelograms, 4 and 5, in the sequence.

3 Statement: *The sum of the angles of a parallelogram is equal to 4 right angles.* True or false? Investigate.

For each parallelogram use a protractor to find the size of the angles and enter your results in a table.

Parallelogram	Angle A	Angle B	Angle C	Angle D	Total
I	108°				
2					
3					
4					
5					

4 a Copy these shapes on to I cm square dot paper.

b Draw the next shape in the sequence.

c Measure the angles.

d Record in a table as in question **3**.

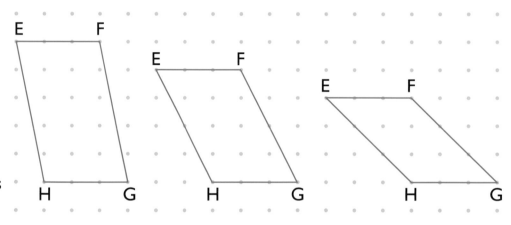

5 Is the general statement true or false? Justify your answer.

1 a Copy these kites and draw the next two kites in the sequence.

b Measure the angles and enter your results in a table.

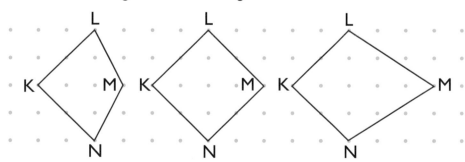

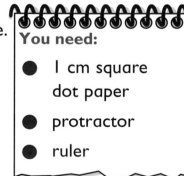

You need:

● I cm square dot paper

● protractor

● ruler

2 Write what you notice about:

a angle K   **b** angles L and N   **c** the sum of the angles in a kite.

Sliding shapes

● **Use properties to identify and draw 2-D shapes**

 1 Name the shape in each overlap of 2 identical equilateral triangles.

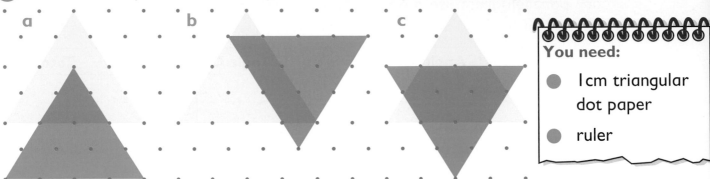

a   b   c

You need:

● 1 cm triangular dot paper

● ruler

2 The diagrams below show the overlap made by 2 identical equilateral triangles.

For each diagram:

● Draw the overlap on 1 cm triangular dot paper.

● Work out how the 2 equilateral triangles were placed to create the overlap and complete each drawing.

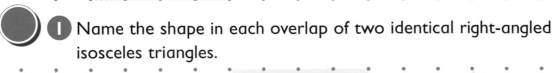

a   b   c   d

 **1** Name the shape in each overlap of two identical right-angled isosceles triangles.

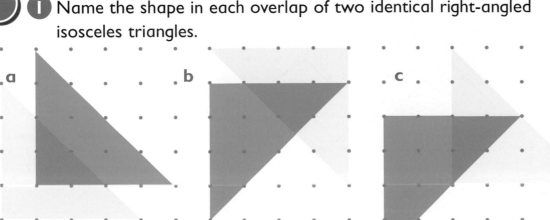

a   b   c

You need:

● 1 cm square dot paper

● ruler

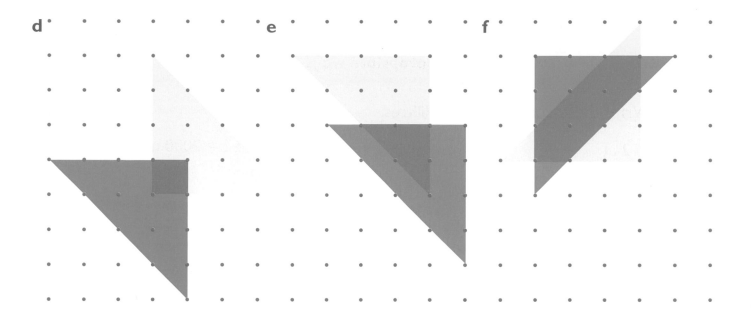

2 Find different overlapping shapes using the same size of triangles as in question **1**.

Record what you find on 1 cm square dot paper.
Remember you can translate, rotate or reflect the triangles.
Here are some ideas:

a rectangle **b** large square

c large parallelogram **d** trapezium

e 2 different pentagons

You have a rectangle and a right-angled triangle.

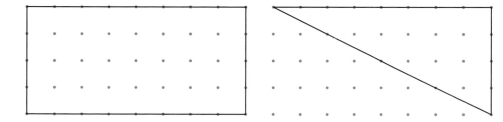

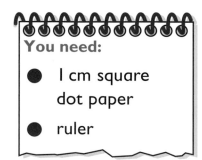

You need:

● 1 cm square dot paper

● ruler

Investigate the different overlapping shapes you can make with these shapes.
Record your overlapping shapes on 1 cm square dot paper.

Measuring capacities

- **Convert larger units to smaller units**
- **Choose and use appropriate number operations to solve problems, and appropriate ways of calculating**

 1 Write these capacities in millilitres.

a $2\frac{1}{2}$ l

b $3\frac{1}{4}$ l

c $4\frac{3}{4}$ l

d $7\frac{1}{10}$ l

e $5\frac{1}{4}$ l

f $6\frac{3}{4}$ l

g $7\frac{1}{2}$ l

h $1\frac{1}{10}$ l

Example

$2\frac{1}{4}$ l = 2000 ml + 250 ml = 2250 ml

2 Write these capacities in litres and millilitres.

a 6250 ml

b 8410 ml

c 6200 ml

d 8400 ml

e 6050 ml

f 8010 ml

g 6020 ml

h 8040 ml

Example

5360 ml = 5000 ml + 360 ml = 5 l + 360 ml

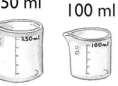

750 ml 500 ml 250 ml 100 ml 50 ml

1 You have these measuring cylinders and an empty container. Remember that you can use each measuring cylinder more than once.

a Write different ways to pour 1 litre of water into the empty container using:
   2 measures
   3 measures
   4 measures
   5 measures

b Write different ways to pour $\frac{1}{2}$ litre of water into the empty container using:
   2 measures
   4 measures
   6 measures

2 You have three measuring jars and an empty container.

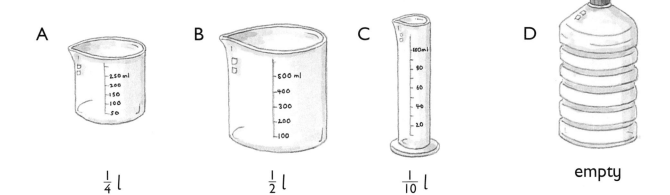

A $\frac{1}{4}l$ B $\frac{1}{2}l$ C $\frac{1}{10}l$ D empty

The table below shows the amounts of water poured into the empty container D. Work out how many millilitres of water container D held each day.

Monday	2 of A	+	3 of B	+	1 of C
Tuesday	4 of A	+	1 of B	+	2 of C
Wednesday	3 of A	+	1 of B	+	5 of C
Thursday	2 of A	+	4 of B	+	6 of C
Friday	5 of A	+	4 of B	+	3 of C

mango
500 ml

pineapple
250 ml

lemon
100 ml

lime 50 ml

1 litre

1 You pour two or more of these measured amounts of fruit juice into an empty one litre jug. Show that you can make 11 different mixed fruit drinks.

2 You top up the jug to the one litre mark with orange juice. How many millilitres of orange juice do you add each time?

Measuring millilitres

Each pair of jugs shows the level before and after some water was added. Write how many millilitres of water is poured into the jug each time.

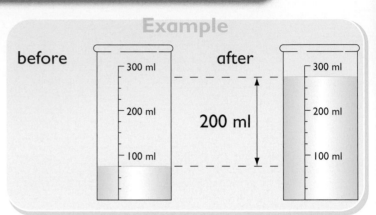

a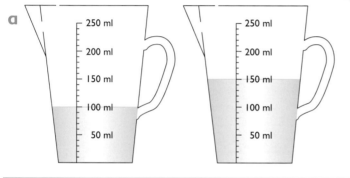

b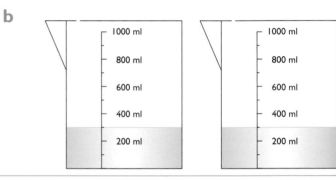

c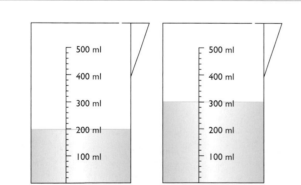

d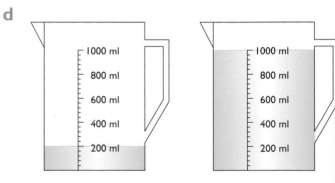

1 200 ml more water is poured into each measuring jar.
Write the new water level.

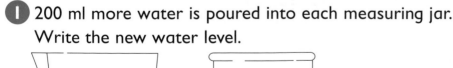

 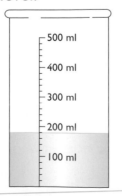 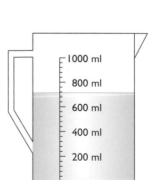 

2 150 ml of water is poured out of each container.
Work out how many millilitres of water are left in each.

a
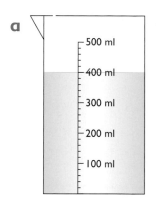

b
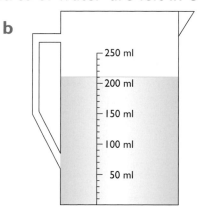

c
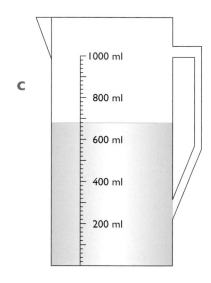

3 Pour water into each jar to raise the level to 1 litre.
Write how many millilitres you add to each jar.

a
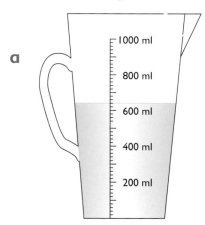

b
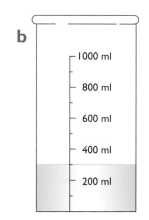

c
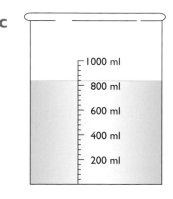

Find a way to measure the amount of vinegar which is added to a jar of pickled onions.
Use marbles for onions and water for vinegar.

Remember

Leave about 1 cm of space at the top of the jar.

Your group needs:

● a clear, uncalibrated plastic bottle or jar (with lid if possible)

● marbles

● funnel

● water

● measuring cylinder

Picnic litres

Use, read and write standard metric units of capacity

Write the pairs of capacities that are the same.
Then find the 'odd one out'.

Example

200 ml = 0·2 l

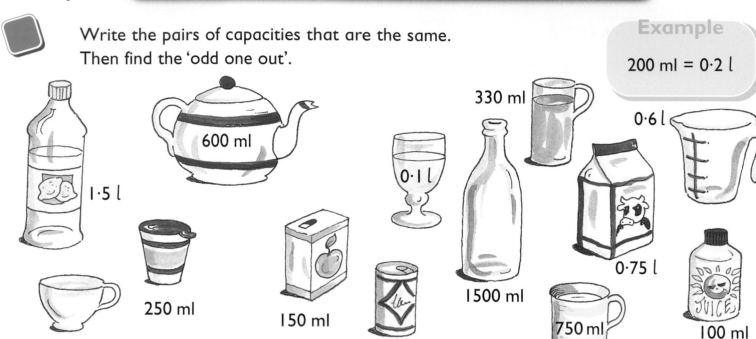

1·5 l

600 ml

330 ml

0·1 l

0·6 l

250 ml

150 ml

1500 ml

0·75 l

0·25 l

0·33 l

750 ml

100 ml

 Some children bought these drinks for a class outing.

orange
250 ml

blackcurrant
220 ml

apple
180 ml

water
500 ml

raspberry
300 ml

lemonade
1500 ml

cola
150 ml

spring
200 ml

cherry
330 ml

1 Change each capacity from millilitres to litres.
Record in decimal form.
Total the capacities. Write the answer in decimal form.

> **Example**
>
> | apple | 180 ml = 0·18 l |
> |---|---|
> | water | 500 ml = 0·5 l |
> | | 680 ml = 0·68 l |

a Andy   orange 250 ml
              water 500 ml

b Beth   blackcurrant 220 ml
             raspberry 300 ml

c Carol   apple 180 ml
             spring 200 ml

d David   lemonade 1500 ml
             cola 150 ml

e Ewan   orange 250 ml
             apple 180 ml

f Fiona   apple 180 ml
            cherry 330 ml

2 Find two soft drinks which make these total capacities:

a 2·0 l   **b** 0·42 l   **c** 1·83 l   **d** 0·58 l

3 Find the total capacity of two cans of cherry and two bottles of lemonade.

Work in a small group.
Find a way to measure
the capacity
of your drinking straw.

Hint:
You may find some
blu-tack or plasticine
helpful.

You need:
● a drinking
straw each
● water
● measuring jar
● beaker
● paper towels

Game results databases

This database shows the results of some games of draughts.

Name	Won	Lost	Drawn
April	3	0	0
Charles	3	1	1
Hoda	4	0	0
Jill	0	5	3
Oliver	1	3	1
Raj	0	2	1
Sam	2	2	0
Tess	2	3	2
Val	1	2	3
Zoë	3	1	1

1 How many games did Jill lose?

2 How many games did Val win?

3 How many games did Charles draw?

4 How many games did Hoda play altogether?

5 Which child won the most games?

6 What is the mode for the number of lost games?

7 What is the mode for the number of drawn games?

8 How many games were won altogether?

9 Who won and lost the same number of games?

Work in groups.

Your group needs:

● a timer

1 Choose a partner and play this game.
Set the timer for 5 minutes. Play as many games as you can.

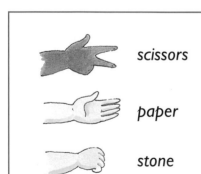

scissors

paper

stone

Both shake your fist three times and make a sign.

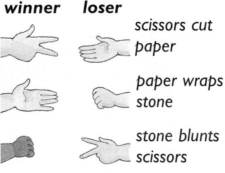

winner   loser

scissors cut paper

paper wraps stone

stone blunts scissors

Decide who wins.

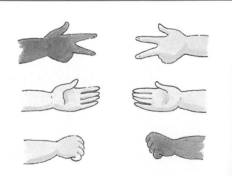

If you make the same sign it's a draw.

2 Record your own results like this. W L L D W W
Use W for Win, L for Lose, D for Draw.

3 Count your wins, losses and draws.

4 Make a database for the group. Each person fills in their results, like this:

Name	Won	Lost	Drawn
Mark	5	7	2

5 Use the information in the database to answer these questions:

a   Who won the most games?

b   Who drew the least number of games?

c   How many children lost more than 5 games?

d   What is the mode for the number of games won?

e   What is the mode for the number of games lost?

f   What is the mode for the number of games drawn?

g   How many games were lost altogether?

h   Who drew more times than they won?

i   How many games were played altogether?

Work in groups.

1 For ten minutes, play the same game as in the ⬤ activity.

2 Record your own results like this.
W(Sc) means you won using scissors.

3 Make a database for the group.

Name	Won	Lost	Drawn	Scissors	Paper	Stone
Mark	5	7	2	6	5	3

Your group needs:
● a timer

4 Calculate the modes for each column.

Liquid line graphs

● Use graphs to answer questions

The table shows the water in a fish pond as Maria filled it.

Time (minutes)	Water (litres)
0	0
5	10
10	15
15	30
20	30
25	30
30	50
35	65
40	70

1 Copy and complete the line graph.

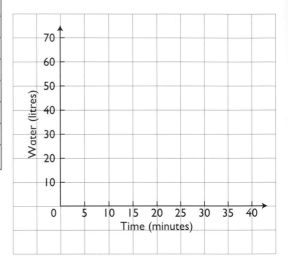

2 a When did the fish pond have 15 litres of water?

b How much water did it take to fill the fish pond?

c How long did it take Maria to fill the pond?

3 Maria took a break after 15 minutes.

a How much water was in the pond then?

b After how many minutes did her break end?

Daniel went on a ten-hour trip. The petrol gauges show the petrol in his car.

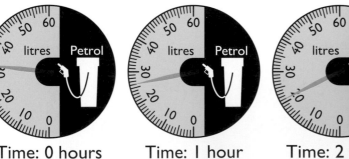

Time: 0 hours   Time: 1 hour   Time: 2 hours   Time: 3 hours   Time: 5 hours

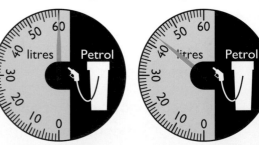

Time: 6 hours   Time: 7 hours   Time: 8 hours   Time: 9 hours   Time: 10 hours

1 Copy and complete the table below.

2 Draw a line graph. Choose scales for the axes to make the graph as easy as possible to read.

3 **a** After how many hours travelling did Daniel fill up his tank with petrol?

Time (hours)	Petrol (litres)
0	
1	
2	
3	

b How much petrol does his tank hold?

c What was the least amount of petrol in his tank?

d How much petrol did he use during the first hour of his trip?

e When do you think Daniel stopped for lunch? Explain your answer.

4 Estimate the petrol in the tank after:

a 8 hours 30 minutes

b 4 hours

5 Estimate when there were 23 litres of petrol in the tank.

The table shows the water in a kettle during the afternoon.

1 Draw a line graph. Choose scales for the axes to make your graph as easy as possible to read.

2 **a** When was the kettle empty?

b When do you think the kettle was full?

c When did the kettle hold less than 300 ml of water?

d How much water was used between 4:00 p.m. and 4:15 p.m.?

e How much water was used between 3:00 p.m. and 3:15 p.m.?

f Estimate the volume of water at 4:05 p.m.

Time (p.m.)	Water (ml)
2:00	200
2:15	0
2:30	0
2:45	600
3:00	350
3:15	120
3:30	120
3:45	600
4:00	390
4:15	0

Travel line graphs

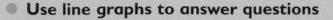

Nazir delivers pizzas on his motorbike. The line graph shows his journey.

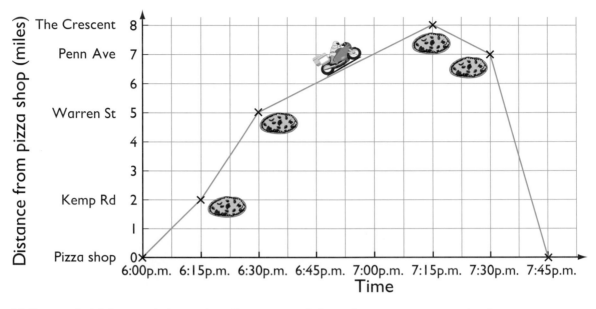

a Where did Nazir deliver his first pizza? At what time was this?
b Where did he deliver his next pizza? When was this?
c When did he deliver a pizza at Penn Avenue?
d Did he deliver a pizza at 7:15 p.m.?
e How far is The Crescent from the pizza shop?

You need:
● graph paper
● ruler

The diagram shows a school trip.

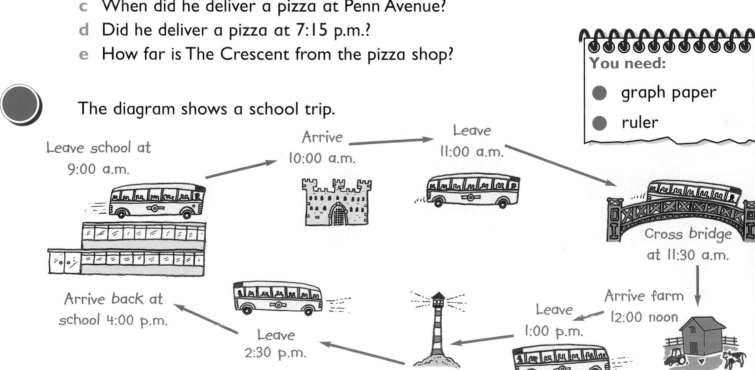

1 a When did the school bus reach the castle?
  b How long did it stay at the castle?
  c When did it leave the castle?
  d When did the bus leave the farm?
  e Where was the bus at 2:30 p.m.?

2 Copy and complete this line graph.

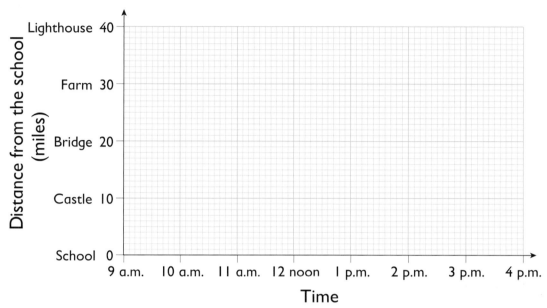

3 a How far is the bridge from the school?
  b How far did the bus travel altogether?
  c How long did the school trip last?
  d How far from school was the bus at 9:30 a.m.?

The line graph shows the journey an aeroplane made one day.

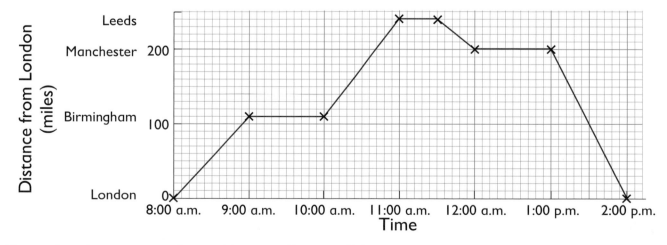

Describe the journey. Begin like this: 'Took off from London at 8:00 a.m.'

Time–distance graphs

● **Use time–distance graphs to answer questions**

 1 This table shows the distances and times for a motorcycle journey from Pilsea to Lissy and back to Pilsea.
Copy and complete the time–distance graph.

You need:
● graph paper   ● ruler

Time (minutes)	Distance from Pilsea (km)
0	0
10	15
20	25
25	35
35	35
45	15
60	0

Motorcycle journey (Pilsea – Lissy – Pilsea)

2 How far was the motorcycle from Pilsea at these times?

a 15 minutes   **b** 30 minutes   **c** 40 minutes   **d** 55 minutes

 This graph shows a train journey for the City Flyer from Welbon to Ibury to Welbon.

You need:
● graph paper   ● ruler

City Flyer

1 When was the City Flyer these distances from Welbon?

a 15 miles going (outward bound)   **b** 18 miles going (outward bound)   **c** 10 miles (return bound)

2 How far was the City Flyer from Welbon at these times?
  a 30 minutes   **b** 5 minutes   **c** 28 minutes   **d** 48 minutes

3 When was the City Flyer not moving?

4 For how long did the City Flyer remain in Ibury?

5 Which train trip is faster: Welborn to Ibury or Ibury to Weldon? How much faster?

6 This table show the distances and times of the Express from Welbon to Ibury.
Copy and complete the time–distance graph.

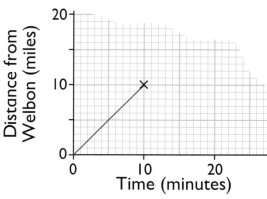

Express

Time (minutes)	Distance from Welbon (miles)
0	0
10	10
15	20
20	20
30	25
35	15
50	0

7 When was the Express these distances from Welbon?
  a 5 miles (outward bound)   **b** 11 miles (outward bound)

8 How far was the Express from Welbon at these times?
  a 25 minutes   **b** 12 minutes

You need:
- graph paper
- ruler
- colouring materials

The diagram shows two spaceships, G2 and K2000, travelling between two space stations.

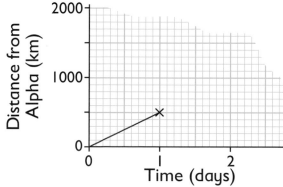

Time (days)	Distance from Alpha (km)	
	G2	**K2000**
0	0	4500
1	500	4000
2	1000	4000
3	3000	3500
4	3000	2000
5	4000	1000
6	4000	1000
7	4500	0

1 Draw a time–distance graph for each spaceship on the same axes.
Use a different colour for each spaceship.

2 Write three statements about the two spaceships.

Investigating heart rate

Collect and organise data to find out about a subject

1 Work in pairs.

Sit down and relax!

Take turns to count the number of times your heart beats in 10 seconds.

While one person counts their heart beats, the other person works the stopwatch.

Measure each person's heart beat five times.

Write the results on a piece of paper.

2 Combine your results and record them on a tally chart.

Heartbeats	Tally	Total

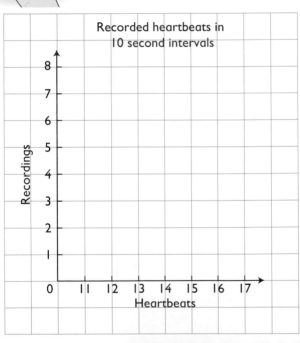

3 What is the mode?

4 Copy and complete the bar line chart.
You may need to start the axes with different numbers from those shown here.

Investigate how long it takes for your heart rate to return to normal after exercise.

2 Sit down and relax. Use a timer to record your pulse for 10 seconds.

(Practise a few times if you need to.)

Multiply the number by 6 to get your heart rate per minute.

Make a note of the number. This is your heart rate when at rest.

2 Copy this table.

3 Run on the spot for about 3 minutes, or as long as you are comfortable with.

Use the stopwatch.

4 Sit down and take your pulse for 10 seconds.

Record your heart rate in the first row of the table.

5 Take your pulse every 2 minutes for 10 minutes.

Record your heart rates in the table.

6 Did your heart rate return to its resting rate after 10 minutes?

7 Draw a line graph to show your results.

Time (minutes)	Heart rate after exercise
0	
2	
4	
6	
8	
10	

You need:

- stopwatch
- graph paper
- ruler

Investigate which activity increases heart rate the most.
Work in a group.

1 Write down a list of exercises that you can perform in the classroom.

2 Decide how you will go about recording the heart rates for the group.

3 Choose two exercises to compare.

Predict which exercise will give the greater heart rate.

4 Decide how much data you need to collect to give a clear result.

Record heart beats for 10 seconds at a time.
Use these numbers to calculate the results.

5 Was your prediction correct?

Remember

You must start off recording your heart beats at rest.

Dice bar line charts

● **Collect and organise data to answer a question**

1 Roll a 1-6 dice 40 times.

Record your results in a tally chart like this.

You need:

● 1 cm squared paper

● 1-6 dice

● ruler

Dice number	Tally	Number of rolls
1		
2		
3		
4		
5		
6		

2 Copy and complete the bar line chart.

3 a How many times did you roll a 3?

b Which number did you roll the most?

c What is this number called?

d How many times did you roll a 1 or 6?

e How many times did you roll an odd number?

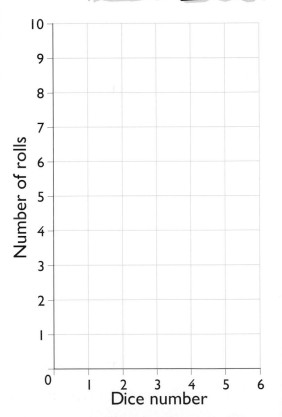

1 Put your counter on the red dot on page 71. Roll your dice to move the counter across that number of dots.

2 Record the numbers the counter touches in a tally chart.

3 When you reach the blue dot, turn around and go back to the red dot.

4 Before you begin, predict which number you think you will record the most. Why?

5 Draw a bar line chart to show your results.

You need:

● 1-6 dice

● counter

● graph paper

● ruler

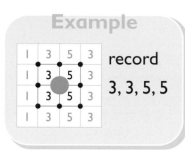

Example

record

3, 3, 5, 5

6	4	2	3	1	3	5	3	6	3
6	4	2	3	1	3	5	3	6	3
6	4	2	3	1	3	5	3	6	3
6	4	2	3	1	3	5	3	6	3
6	4	2	3	1	3	5	3	6	3
6	4	2	3	1	3	5	3	6	3

6 a Which number did you record most?

b What is this number called?

c How many times did you land on a number greater than 3?

d Which number has the lowest frequency? How does your chart show this?

7 Make up another way to use the grid. Do the activity and record your results.

Work in a group.

1 Examine the dice in the box. Which number do you think is most likely to be on top most often?

2 Take turns to empty the box of dice on to the table. Record the results of the dice numbers that are on top in a tally chart.

3 Each person draws a bar line chart.

4 a What is the mode?

b What is the frequency of the mode?

c How many numbers greater than the mode were on top?

d How many numbers less than the mode were on top?

5 If you emptied the box of dice again, which number do you think would come up most? Try it and see.

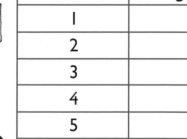

Dice number	Tally	Total
1		
2		
3		
4		
5		
6		

You need:

● box of dice (per group)

● graph paper (per child)

● ruler (per child)

Spinners

- Collect and organise data to answer a question
- Describe how likely an event is to happen

 Work in a group.

1 Look at the spinner. Predict how many red numbers you would expect to get in 100 spins.

2 Copy the tally chart and place it in the middle of your group.

Colour	Tally	Total
red		
green		

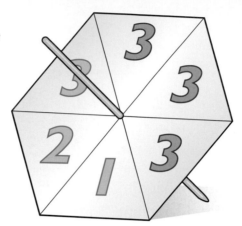

You need:
- pencil
- paper clip
- 1 cm squared paper

3 Spin your spinner. Use a tally mark to record the colour it lands on.

Make 100 tally marks altogether.

4 Find the total spins for each colour. How close was your prediction?

5 Copy and complete the pictogram.

Spinner results

red	
green	

○ stands for _____ spins

 Work in pairs.

Design a six-sided spinner. Follow these rules:

- Use the numbers 1, 2 and 3 to number your spinner.

- Number your spinner so that 3 has an even chance of being spun.

- Write each number in red or blue, but red must have a good chance of being spun.

You need:
- blank six-sided spinner (per pair)
- red and blue coloured pencils (per pair)
- 1 cm squared paper or graph paper (per person)
- ruler (per person)

2 Copy these tally charts.

Colour	Tally	Total

Number	Tally	Total

3 Before you begin make some predictions. Spin the spinners and record 100 tally marks in each tally chart.

4 Are the results what you expected? Explain your answers.

5 Draw a chart for each set of data.

Design an 8-sided spinner. Work in pairs.

Follow these rules:
- Use the numbers 1, 2, 3, 4. You do not have to use all of them.
- Write the numbers in red, green or blue. You must use all three colours.

1 Write down the chance of each number being spun.

2 Write down the chance of each colour being spun.

3 Spin the spinner 40 times.

4 Record your results using tally charts.

5 Are the results as you expected? Explain why.

6 Draw charts to present your data.

You need:
- blank eight-sided spinner (per pair)
- red, blue and green coloured pencils (per pair)
- I cm squared paper or graph paper (per child)
- ruler (per child)

Gardeners' questions

 Work out the following gardening questions, show all your working out.

a How many apples and pears has the gardener picked?

b How many more pears does he need to have 200 altogether?

c He has already sold 65 plums, how many did he start with?

d If the number of pears he had doubled, how many would he have?

e How much fruit does he have altogether?

Work out the following gardening questions, show all your working out.

a How many tulips and snowdrops does the gardener have altogether?

b If the gardener needs a total of 500 tulips how many more does he need?

c The gardener has already planted 372 crocuses, how many did he have to start with?

d The gardener started with 731 snowdrops, how many has he planted so far?

e The gardener decides that he wants to have a total of 850 snowdrops and tulips. How many more does he need?

f How many bulbs does he have altogether?

g Make up two word problems for your partner to work out. You must work out the answer before you give the problem to them.

The gardener's friend tells him he has 2 tulip bulbs for every 4 snowdrop bulbs.

a If he has 870 bulbs altogether, how many of each does he have?

b If he has spent £96 on all the bulbs, how much did he spend on tulips?

Calculating costs

Use a calculator to solve problems involving decimals

 £65

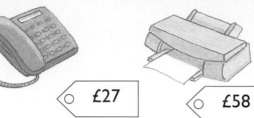 £27

 £58

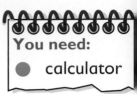 £327

1 Use your calculator to find the total cost. Show all your working.

a Two mobile phones and a printer
b Three telephones and a computer
c Four printers, a computer and telephone
d Two mobile phones and three printers

27p   48p   92p   83p

2 Use your calculator to find the total cost in £ and p. Show all your working.

a Four pencils and an eraser
b A sharpener and three rulers
c Two erasers and two pencils
d Five sharpeners and two rulers

 £6·48

 £4·25

 £8·52

 96p

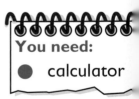

1 Use your calculator to find the total cost. Show all your working.

a A calculator and two organisers
b Three computer mice and a stapler
c Two organisers and two computer mice
d Five staplers and 4 calculators
e Two computer mice, two organisers and two calculators

2 Now work out these.

a How much more is a mouse than an organiser?

b How much more are three organisers than a mouse?

c How much more is a calculator than a stapler?

d How much more are seven staplers than an organiser?

3 Calculate the cost in two different ways.

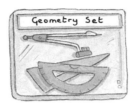

pen £1.34
pencil 90p

stapler £2.28
staples 75p

compasses £1.97
protractor 75p

a Four geometry sets

b Two pen and pencil sets

c Three stapler packs

d Four geometry sets and a stapler pack

e Five pen and pencil sets and two stapler packs

Example

Find the cost of two geometry sets
Two compasses cost
  2 × £1.97 =   £3.94
Two protractors cost
  2 × 75p =   £1.50
Total cost   =   £5.44

Compasses and protractor cost
  £1.97 + 75p =   £2.72
2 geometry sets cost
  2 × £2.72 =   £5.44

 £29

 £44

 £53

 £19

1 Use both of the methods shown to work out the cost of these items.

a Three satchels and a suitcase

b A handbag and three briefcases

c A briefcase and two suitcases

d Five suitcases and a satchel

2 Write down a rule for when the calculator method works.

Example

Find the cost of four handbags and a suitcase.

Written or mental method

Four handbags cost:
      4 × £19 =   £76
    A suitcase costs: £53
      Total cost =   £129

Using a calculator

Four handbags and a suitcase costs:
      4 × £19 + £53

[4] [×] [1] [9] [+] [5] [3]   129.

Total cost = £129

Reviewing multiplication and division

Example

356 × 8 → 350 × 8 = 2800

×	300	50	6
8	2400	400	48

    2400
     400
  +   48
    ────
    2848

or

```
      356
    ×   8
     2400   (300 × 8)
      400   ( 50 × 8)
       48   (  6 × 8)
     ────
     2848
```

or

```
     356
   ×   8
    2848
     4 4
```

- Choose one number from the rectangle and one number from the circle.
- Estimate what the product of these two numbers is and write it down.
- Then multiply the two numbers together. Show all your working.
- Your teacher will tell you how many calculations to do.

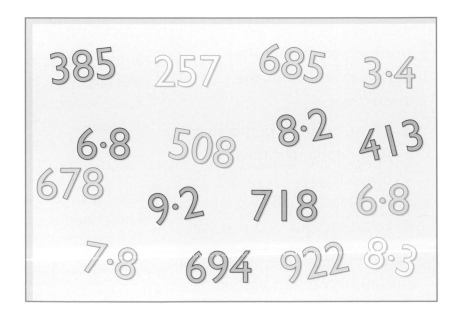

Example

$36 \times 84 \rightarrow 35 \times 80 = 2800$

×	30	6
80	2400	480
4	120	24

2400
480
120
+ 24
3024
| |

or

36
× 84
2880
144
3024
| |

80 × 36
4 × 36

- Choose one number from the rectangle and one number from the oval.
- Estimate what the product of these two numbers is and write it down.
- Then multiply the two numbers together. Show all your working.
- Your teacher will tell you how many calculations to do.

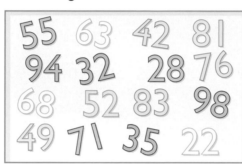

Example

$534 \div 7 \rightarrow 560 \div 7 = 80$

534		or	7) 534		or	76 R2

534
− 490   (70 × 7)
44
− 42   (6 × 7)
2
Answer: 76 R2

or   7) 534
− 490   (70 × 7)
44
− 42   (6 × 7)
2
Answer: 76 R2

or   76 R2
7) 534
− 49
44
− 42
2

- Choose one number from the rectangle and one number from the circle.
- Make a HTU ÷ U calculation, estimate the answer and write it down.
- Then work out the answer. Show all your working.
- Your teacher will tell you how many calculations to do.

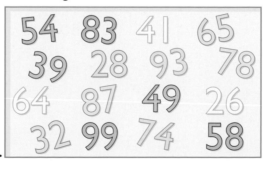

Calculator error

● **Develop calculator skills and use a calculator effectively**

 ① Round these numbers to the nearest whole number.

a	2.9999998	b	0.9999999	c	21.999999
d	10.999998	e	9.9999999	f	50.999999
g	46.999999	h	29.999999	i	99.999999

You need:
● calculator

② Calculate the answer. Round it to the nearest whole number.

a 8 × 1·999999

b 7 × 9·9999999

c 25 × 0·9999999

d 11 × 10·9999999

e 2 × 19·999999

f 9 × 99·999999

Example

5 × 2·9999999 = | 14.999999 |
round to 15

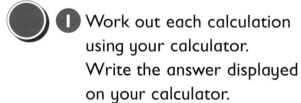 ① Work out each calculation using your calculator. Write the answer displayed on your calculator. Write the answer to the nearest whole number.

Example

2 ÷ 6 × 3

Calculator display	Rounded answer
0.9999999	1

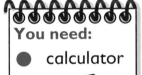

You need:
● calculator

a 4 ÷ 3 × 3

b 2 ÷ 3 × 12

c 8 ÷ 12 × 3

d 25 ÷ 15 × 3

e 7 ÷ 6 × 18

f 32 ÷ 48 × 6

g 250 ÷ 90 × 9

h 11 ÷ 12 × 36

i 10 ÷ 30 × 15

j 64 ÷ 48 × 6

k 17 ÷ 9 × 72

l 500 ÷ 300 × 150

m 1000 ÷ 90 × 900

n 2 ÷ 600 × 1800

o 48 ÷ 36 × 9

c Netballs now cost half of their original price. How much money do you save by buying 16 balls in the sale?

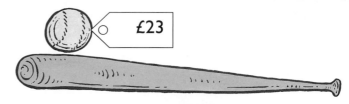

£23

d The golf club has three instructors. Each instructor has bookings for three one-hour lessons and five $\frac{1}{2}$-hour lessons per day. Each instructor works seven days a week. How much money does the club take in golf lesson bookings in a week?

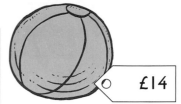

£14

e Mrs Jonson buys eight baseball bat sets for her class. How much change does she receive from £200?

£47

f The after-school club buys two of every item shown, but not any golf lessons. How much do they spend?

Golf lessons £13 per hour

1 Use the prices of the sports items on these two pages to write your own word problems for these calculations. Approximate the answer first (if necessary).

a (7 × £2·50) + (2 × £39) **b** (6 × 57) + (12 × 13) **c** 14 × ($\frac{1}{2}$ × 13)

d (10 × 47) − 47 **e** 16 × 23 + 47 **f** 16 × (23 + 47)

2 Calculate the answer using the most appropriate method. You may use a calculator.

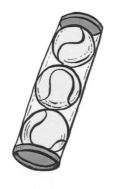
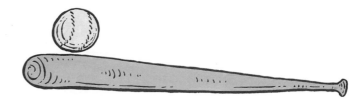

Banquet litres

In the Elizabethan kitchen of Burghley House, the copper pots and saucepans are hung in a row.

a   b   c   d   e   f

2·2 l   3·7 l   5·5 l   6·8 l   7·9 l   9·1 l

Round the capacity of each pot and saucepan to the nearest litre.

Example

4·6 l = 5 l to nearest litre

1 The cook has prepared 40 litres of chicken soup for the starter course. Each soup plate is 250 ml.

   a How many guests can have a plate of soup?

   b Only 120 guests take the soup. How many litres of soup are left over for the kitchen staff?

2 The recipe for tomato sauce is:
5 tomatoes make 500 ml of sauce.

   a How much sauce can the kitchen boy make with 25 tomatoes?

   b The cook orders him to make 5 litres of sauce. How many tomatoes will he need?

3 Look at the pots in the ▢ activity. The assistant cook uses pots **d** and **e** to boil vegetables.
What is the total capacity of the pots?

4 The pantry maid is filling the butter churn with milk.

A full churn holds 7·5 litres.

A full jug holds 500 ml.

How many jugs of milk will fill the churn?

5 The copper cauldron holds 60 litres of hot water. The brass urn holds $2\frac{1}{2}$ times as much.

a How many litres does the brass urn hold?

b The scullery maid uses 18 litres of hot water from the urn to wash dishes. How many litres of water does the urn now hold?

These old storage jars all contain some olive oil. The amount in each higher jar is the sum of the two jars below.

1 How many litres of olive oil are in the top jar?

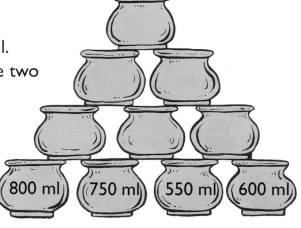

800 ml 750 ml 550 ml 600 ml

2 The bottom row jars shown below can go in any order.

How many top jar capacities can you have by arranging the bottom row of jars in different ways?

700 ml   650 ml   750 ml   500 ml

Using square units

- Know that area is measured in cm²
- Use the formula 'length × breadth' for the area of a rectangle

1 Draw these rectangles on 1 cm squared paper. Find the area of each rectangle.

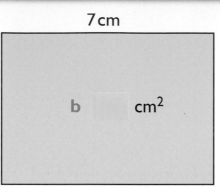

7 cm

5 cm

b ___ cm²

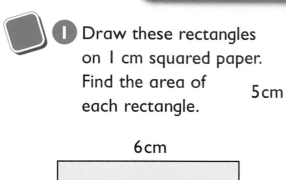

6 cm

3 cm

a ___ cm²

11 cm

6 cm

c ___ cm²

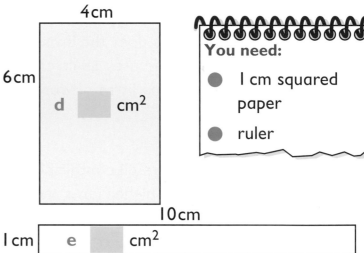

4 cm

6 cm

d ___ cm²

You need:
- 1 cm squared paper
- ruler

10 cm

1 cm   e ___ cm²

Size of square	
1 square millimetre	1 mm²
1 square centimetre	1 cm²
1 square metre	1 m²

1 square millimetre or 1 mm²

1 Write which size of square you would use to measure the area of:

a the front cover of this Pupil book
b the board
c a petal of a daisy
d a football pitch

e a computer key
f a slice of bread
g your thumbnail
h the school hall

2 Find the area of each of these.
Remember to answer in square units.

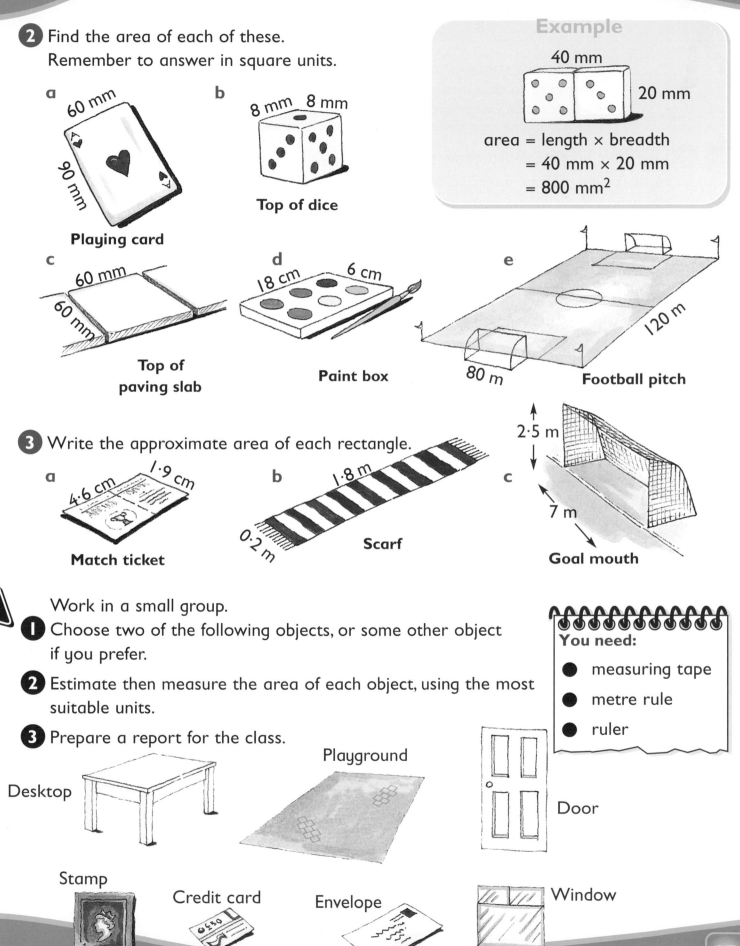

Example

40 mm

20 mm

area = length × breadth
= 40 mm × 20 mm
= 800 mm²

a
60 mm
90 mm
Playing card

b
8 mm 8 mm
Top of dice

c
60 mm
60 mm
Top of paving slab

d
18 cm 6 cm
Paint box

e
120 m
80 m
Football pitch

3 Write the approximate area of each rectangle.

a
1·9 cm
4·6 cm
Match ticket

b
1·8 m
0·2 m
Scarf

c
2·5 m
7 m
Goal mouth

Work in a small group.

1 Choose two of the following objects, or some other object if you prefer.

2 Estimate then measure the area of each object, using the most suitable units.

3 Prepare a report for the class.

You need:
● measuring tape
● metre rule
● ruler

Desktop

Playground

Door

Stamp

Credit card

Envelope

Window

87

Drawing angles

- **Use a protractor to measure and draw acute and obtuse angles to the nearest 5°**
- **Calculate angles in a straight line**

1 Use your protractor to draw these right angles in your exercise book. Mark the right angle each time.

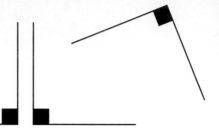

You need:
- circular protractor
- ruler

2 Draw these acute angles. Mark each angle with an arc and write its size.

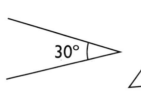
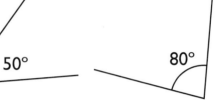

3 In the same way, draw these obtuse angles.

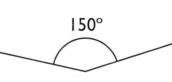

straight line 180°

right angle 90°

acute angle between 0° and 90°

obtuse angle between 90° and 180°

1 Draw and label these acute angles.

a	50°	b	70°
c	25°	d	55°
e	85°	f	20°

2 Draw and label two right angles.

3 Draw and label these obtuse angles.

a	120°	b	160°
c	135°	d	95°
e	105°	f	170°

Example

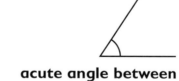

You need:
- protractor
- ruler

Example

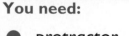

88

4 Copy these diagrams.
Calculate the size of angles **a** to **c**.
Check with your protractor.

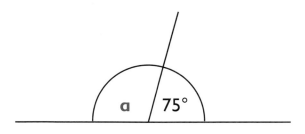

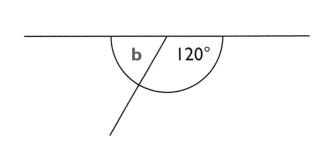

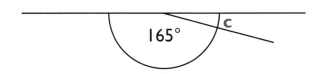

Angles in a clock face

1 Find a way to draw this clock face.

You can begin by:
● drawing round a large plastic circle
● using a pair of compasses to draw the circle.

Mark the centre of the circle.

Draw angle arms to each of the hours.

Number the hours 1 to 12.

2 Calculate the obtuse angle between the hands at:
a 4 o'clock **b** 5 o'clock.

3 At the half hour, the hour hand is halfway
between the hours.
Draw and measure:
a the acute angle at 3:30
b the obtuse angle at 9:30.

4 Work out the size of the remaining 10 acute or obtuse
angles for the half hour times between 1:30 and 12:30.

You need:

● ruler

● large plastic circle or pair
of compasses

● protractor

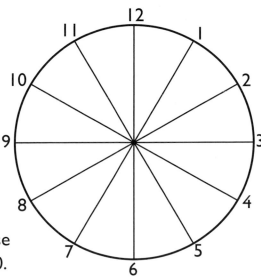

Grid positions

- **Complete symmetrical patterns with two lines of symmetry at right angles**
- **Use co-ordinates to translate a shape**

① Check that this pattern has two lines of symmetry. Place your mirror on the dashed lines.

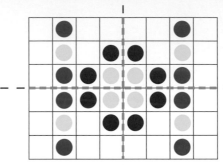

② Copy each grid on to squared paper.

Draw the two lines of symmetry with dashed lines.
Use four colours.
Reflect and complete each pattern.

Remember

Check with a mirror.

a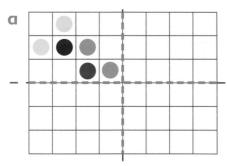

b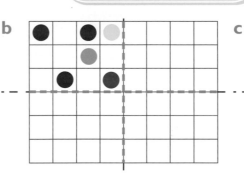

c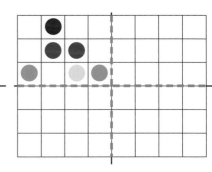

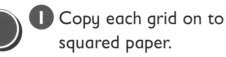

① Copy each grid on to squared paper.

Draw the two lines of symmetry with dashed lines.

Example

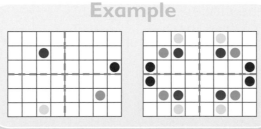

Mark the position of each peg as shown.
Reflect each peg, in turn, into the other three sectors and complete your pattern.

a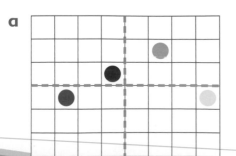

b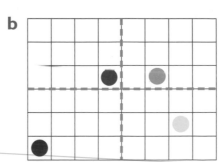

c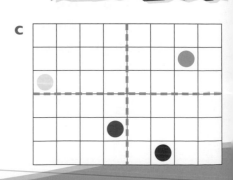

d 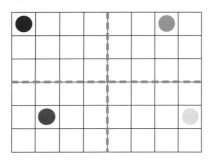   e 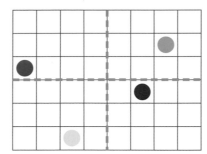   f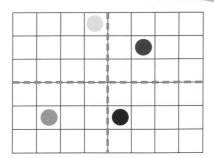

2 The co-ordinates of shape A are:
(0, 2), (0, 6), (2, 5), (2, 3).

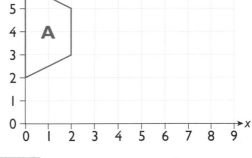

a Add 3 units to the first number in A's
co-ordinates to make shape B.
Copy and complete: (3, 2) (3, 6) (▢, 5) (▢, 3)
Plot the points and join them in order.

b Add 6 units to the first number in A's
co-ordinates to make shape C. Copy and
complete: (6, 2) (▢, 6) (▢, ▢) (▢, ▢)
Plot the points and join them in order.

c Copy and complete:
Shape A has been translated ▢ units to the ▢▢▢ to make shape C.

1 The co-ordinates of shape A are: (1, 4) (2, 5) (4, 4) (5, 2) (4, 1) (2, 2)
Add 3 units each time to the first co-ordinate of shape A.
Copy and complete:
Shape B (4, 4) (5, 5) (▢, 4) (▢, 2) (▢, 1) (▢, 2)
Shape C (7, 4) (8, 5) (▢, 4) (▢, 2) (▢, 1) (▢, 2)
Shape D (10, 4) (11, 5) (▢, ▢) (▢, ▢) (▢, ▢) (▢, ▢)
Plot these points on the grid and join them in order.

You need:
● I cm squared
paper

2 Add 3 units each time to the second co-ordinate
of shape A. Copy and complete:
Shape E (1, 7) (2, 8) (4, ▢) (2, ▢) (▢, ▢) (▢, ▢)
Shape F (1, 10) (2, 11) (▢, ▢) (▢, ▢)
(▢, ▢) (▢, ▢)
The shape translates 3 units up each time.
Plot these points and join them in order.

3 Continue the translating pattern to the right and
up until you have filled the grid.
Use two colours to show your repeating pattern.

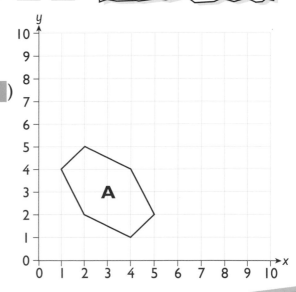

Making connections

This is the winter timetable for Friday flights between London Heathrow and Glasgow. The flight takes 1 hour and 15 minutes.

a Copy and complete the timetable.

b The 10:55 flight is delayed by 20 minutes. At what time will it leave London?

c What is the new arrival time in Glasgow?

Depart London	Arrive Glasgow
07:05	
09:00	10:15
10:55	
	14:10
15:30	
	18:15
19:15	
	23:00

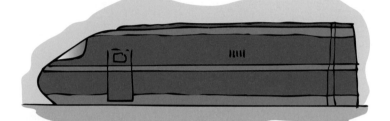

1 This is a bus timetable from Cambridge to Luton Airport. Buses leave every two hours.

a Copy and complete the bus timetable.

b How long is the bus journey from Cambridge to Luton Airport?

c You need to arrive at the airport just before quarter past 2. Which bus would you catch at Baldock?

d The 17:00 bus is 17 minutes late at Royston. At what time does it arrive?

Cambridge	11:00	13:00	15:00	17:00
Trumpington	11:10	13:10		
Harston	11:15	13:15		
Royston	11:25	13:25		
Baldock	11:40			
Letchworth	11:42			
Hitchin	11:50			
Luton Airport	12:05	14:05	16:05	18:05

2 This table shows some of the train times from Kings Cross to Luton Airport.

Kings Cross	16:01	16:16	16:19	16:34	16:46	17:04
Luton Airport	16:31	16:46	17:02	17:04	17:16	17:37

a The Express train takes exactly 30 minutes for the journey.
Which of the above times from Kings Cross are for Express trains?

b If you catch the 16:19 train, how long is the journey to Luton Airport in minutes?

c At what time does the slowest train leave Kings Cross?

d Your holiday flight departs from Luton Airport at 19:35.
You need to allow 15 minutes for the bus shuttle from the station to the airport.
You must check in two hours before departure.
Which train should you catch at Kings Cross?

Your friend is planning a holiday to Palma.
She is having difficulty in reading the timetable.
She wants to fly to Palma on a Saturday in June and return home on a Sunday flight two weeks later.
She wants to fly during daytime and likes a window seat.
Look at the timetable. Decide which is the best outward and return flight.
Write them in the 12-hour clock.

Day	Luton to Palma			Palma to Luton		
	Flt. no.	Dep.	Arr.	Flt. no.	Dep.	Arr.
Mon–Fri	401	12:35	16:00	402	16:50	20:20
Mon–Fri	419	21:40	01:05	418*	01:45	05:15
Sat	407	10:40	14:05	406	14:45	18:15
Sat	401	12:35	16:00	402	16:50	20:20
Sat	409	17:05	20:30	408	21:10	00:40
Sat	421	21:15	00:40			
Sun				424	01:20	04:50
Sun	413	06:20	09:45	412	10:25	13:55
Sun	401	12:35	16:00	402	16:50	20:20
*Except Monday						

Skittle fractions

 Work out these fractions. The first one is done for you.

 Example

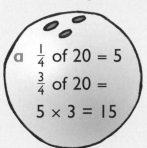

a $\frac{1}{4}$ of 20 = 5
$\frac{3}{4}$ of 20 =
5 × 3 = 15

First I need to find $\frac{1}{4}$, then I can work out $\frac{3}{4}$.

b $\frac{1}{3}$ of 30
$\frac{2}{3}$ of 30

c $\frac{1}{5}$ of 50
$\frac{2}{5}$ of 50

d $\frac{1}{4}$ of £200
$\frac{3}{4}$ of £200

e $\frac{1}{5}$ of 100 litres
$\frac{3}{5}$ of 100 litres

f $\frac{1}{3}$ of 60 m
$\frac{2}{3}$ of 60 m

g $\frac{1}{4}$ of 80
$\frac{3}{4}$ of 80

h $\frac{1}{4}$ of 400 km
$\frac{3}{4}$ of 400 km

i $\frac{1}{3}$ of £75
$\frac{2}{3}$ of £75

j $\frac{1}{5}$ of 125 kg
$\frac{4}{5}$ of 125 kg

1 Find the fractions of these numbers.

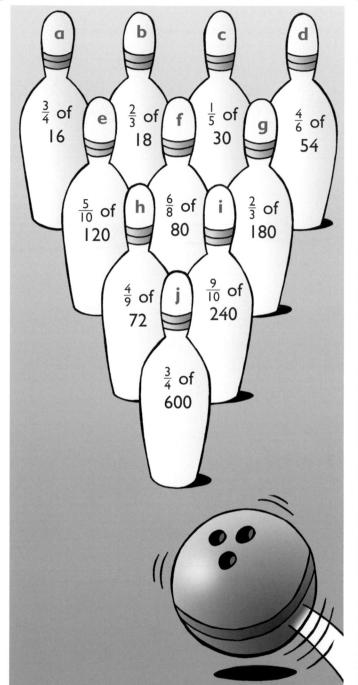

a $\frac{3}{4}$ of 16
b $\frac{2}{3}$ of 18
c $\frac{1}{5}$ of 30
d $\frac{4}{6}$ of 54
e
f
g
h
i
j
$\frac{5}{10}$ of 120
$\frac{6}{8}$ of 80
$\frac{2}{3}$ of 180
$\frac{4}{9}$ of 72
$\frac{9}{10}$ of 240
$\frac{3}{4}$ of 600

2 Find the fractions of these quantities.

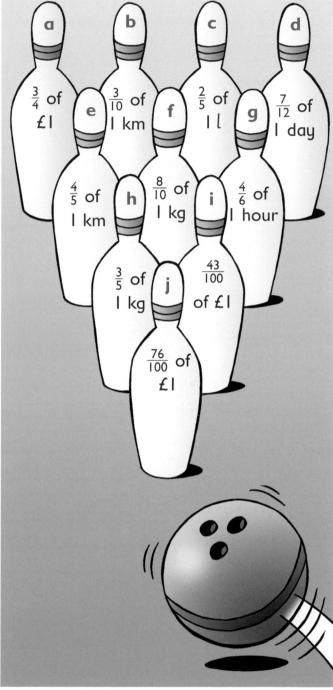

a $\frac{3}{4}$ of £1
b $\frac{3}{10}$ of 1 km
c $\frac{2}{5}$ of 1 l
d $\frac{7}{12}$ of 1 day
e
f
g
h
i
j
$\frac{4}{5}$ of 1 km
$\frac{8}{10}$ of 1 kg
$\frac{4}{6}$ of 1 hour
$\frac{3}{5}$ of 1 kg
$\frac{43}{100}$ of £1
$\frac{76}{100}$ of £1

What fraction?

a What fraction of £1 is 70p?
b What fraction of 1 km is 750 m?
c What fraction of 1 litre is 200 ml?
d What fraction of a day is 16 hours?
e What fraction of an hour is 10 minutes?

f What fraction of 1 m is 70 cm?
g What fraction of £1 is 45p?
h What fraction of 1 kg is 800 g?
i What fraction of a minute is 40 seconds?
j What fraction of 1 km is 400 m?

Fractions and decimals

● **Relate fractions to their decimal equivalent**

 1 Look at the number lines. What are the missing fractions and decimals?

a

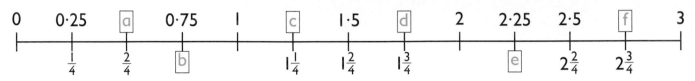

b

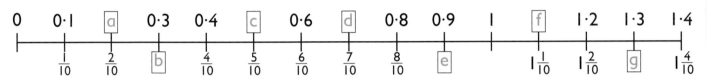

2 Quick pointer

Play with a partner.

Take it in turns to point to one of the fractions or decimals.

Your partner must point to the equivalent fraction or decimal.

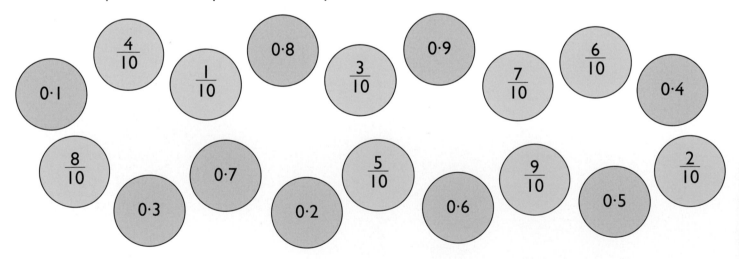

1 Look at the number lines. What are the missing fractions and decimals?

a

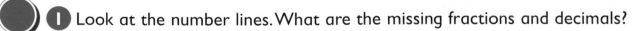
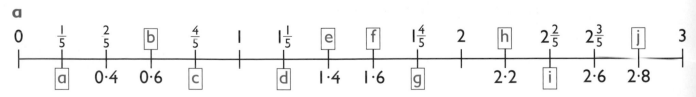

b

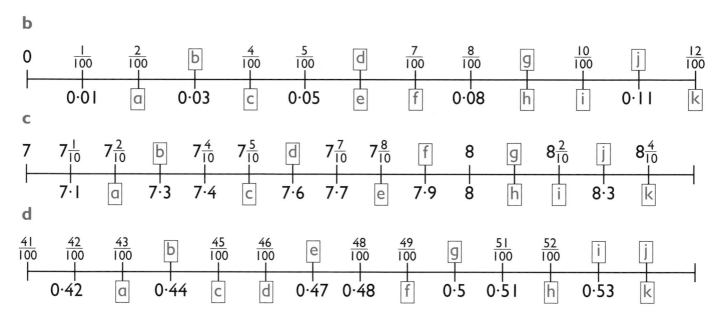

c

d

2 Quick pointer

Play with a partner.

Take it in turns to point to one of the fractions or decimals.

Your partner must point to the equivalent fraction or decimal.

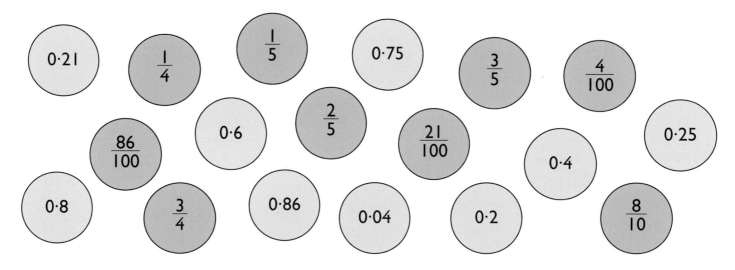

What are the numbers?

a I am thinking of a number: 0.2 of it is 12.

b I am thinking of a number: $\frac{28}{100}$ of it is 14.

c I am thinking of a number: 0.75 of it is 51.

d I am thinking of a number: $\frac{6}{10}$ of it is 156.

e I am thinking of a number: 0.25 of it is 34.

Pizza problems

Represent a problem by identifying the information needed to solve it, find possible solutions and confirm them in the context of the problem

PERFECT PIZZAS

Cheese and tomato	buy it in quarters
Ham and mushroom	buy it in halves

How much pizza did each of these children buy?

a   Tilly buys 1 slice of ham and mushroom pizza and 2 slices of cheese and tomato pizza.

b   Henry buys 3 slices of cheese and tomato and 1 slice of ham and mushroom pizza.

PERFECT PIZZAS

Cheese and tomato	buy it in quarters
Ham and mushroom	buy it in thirds
Vegetarian	buy it in sixths
Pepperoni	buy it in eighths

How much pizza did each of these children buy?

a Tom buys 2 slices of vegetarian pizza and 1 slice of ham and mushroom pizza.

b Hannah buys 2 slices of cheese and tomato and 3 slices of pepperoni pizza.

c Alex buys 5 slices of vegetarian pizza and 1 slice of ham and mushroom pizza.

d Julia buys 1 slice of cheese and tomato pizza and 5 slices of pepperoni pizza.

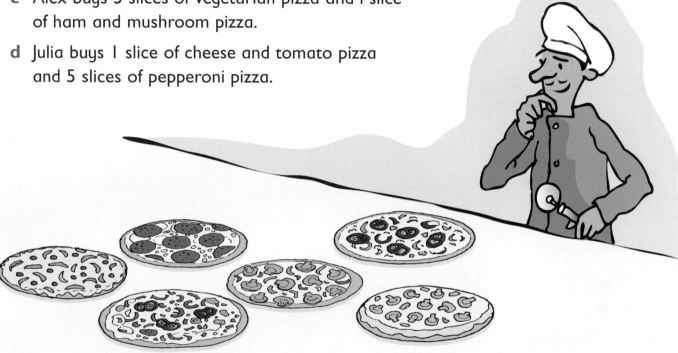

 Look at the pizzas in the activity. Joe buys 2 slices of vegetarian and 3 slices of pepperoni pizza. How much pizza did he buy altogether?

HINT

To change them to the same fraction you have to find another fraction that you can change sixths and eighths into.

Shop percentages

Understand percentage as the number of parts in every 100

Find 50% and 25% of these amounts.

Remember
50% is half.
25% is one quarter.

12 grapefruit

20 pears

16 oranges

8 melons

24 apples

40 bananas

48 plums

80 cherries

44 satsumas

60 strawberries

1 Work out 10% of these prices.

a £12
b £26
c £9
d £21
e £30
f £64
g £15
h £92
i £108
j £120

2 Work out 1% of these prices.

a DAB Radio £200

b CD/MP3 player £120

c MP3 Player £100

d DVD recorder £240

e HD DVD Player £400

f 22" LCD TV £320

g 100 Re-recordable DVDs £160

h BluRay Player £220

i Video phone £180

j 42" Plasma screen £1000

Find 15% of all the prices in the ⬤ activity.

Example

1% of £120 = £1.20 (£1.20 × 15 = £18)

Race to 100%

What percentage of the shapes on the children's jumpers are red?

a

b

c

d

e

f

g

h

i

j

Race to 100%

Play the game in twos or threes.

● Take it in turns to roll the dice and colour in that per cent of your grid. For example, roll a 6 and colour 6% of your grid.

● The winner is the first player to colour all of their grid. Remember you must be able to colour 100% exactly with your last throw!

You need:

● blank 10 x 10 grid each

● 1-10 dice

● coloured pencil each

Bonus Percentages

7% 25% 38% 51%
70% 85% 94%
Get these and you have
an extra throw.

I have got 25% so I
can have another go!

Play the game
Race to 100% in
the ⬤ activity on
a 200 square.

Before you play,
work out what is
1% of the grid.

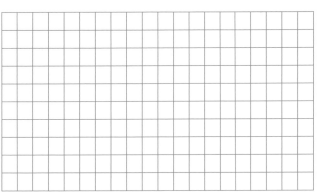

You need:
- ⬤ 20 × 10 grid
  each
- ⬤ coloured pencil
  each

Fractions, decimals and percentages again

● **Understand equivalence between simple fractions, decimals and percentages**

 Choosing one sweet from each jar, match the equivalent fractions, decimals and percentages.

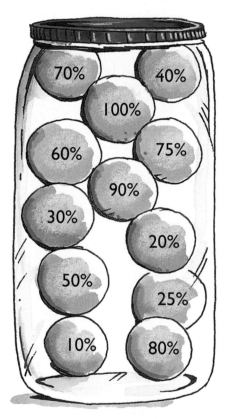

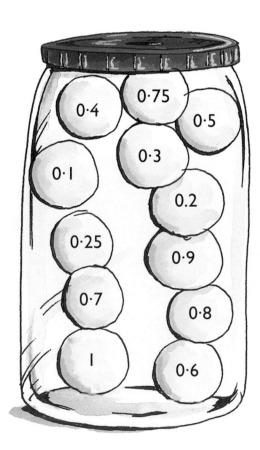

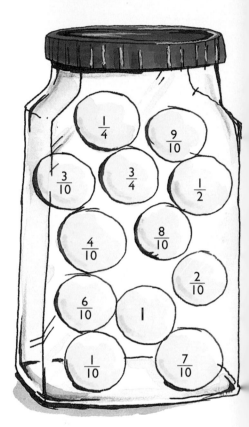

Copy and complete the table.

Fraction	Percentage	Decimal
	10%	
$\frac{75}{100}$		
		0·24
	80%	
		0·25
	20%	
		0·9
	40%	
		0·01
$\frac{53}{100}$		

2 Look at the percentages that are in **red**.
They have another equivalent fraction. What is it?

 Design a domino set where equivalent fractions and percentages are matched.
If you have time make the dominoes out of card and play the game.

25% | $\frac{48}{100}$

$\frac{1}{4}$ | 2%

50% | $\frac{8}{10}$

30% | $\frac{7}{10}$

Running problems

● Solve one-step and two-step problems involving whole numbers and decimals, choosing and using appropriate calculation strategies

These are the times for some runners in a half marathon. Look at the table and answer the questions below. Show all your working.

a Put the runners' names in order from fastest to slowest.

b What is the difference in time between the fastest and the slowest runners?

c What is the difference in time between Sara and Samuel?

d What is the total of all the girls' times?

e What is the total of all the boys' times?

Name	Time (minutes)
Samuel	186
Sara	231
Stuart	204
Shantie	193
Selina	172
Simon	257

Look at the table of some children's running times. Then work out the answers to the problems below. Show all your working.

a Put the runners' names in order from fastest to slowest.

b What is the difference in time between the fastest and the slowest runners?

c What is the difference in time between Max and Molly?

Name	Time (minutes)
Megan	4·22
Max	3·96
Mark	4·58
Molly	4·37
Madeleine	3·87
Martin	4·03

d What is the total of all the girls' times?

e What is the difference between all the girls' times and all the boys' times?

f Whose time is closest to 4·3 minutes?

g The sports teacher says 'I want everyone to aim for a time of 4·2 minutes.' Which runners need to run faster and by how much?

 Round each runner's time from the ⬤ activity to one decimal place, and then work out their time in seconds.

Example

Megan's time is rounded to 4·2 minutes.
   4 minutes is 240 seconds.
   0·2 of a minute is 12 seconds.
   Her time in seconds is 252 seconds.

Remember

0·1 of a minute is $\frac{1}{10}$ of a minute, which is 6 seconds.

Summer Fair fun

● Solve one-step and two-step problems involving whole numbers and decimals, choosing and using appropriate calculation strategies

 1 Work out these calculations using your calculator.

a £25.12 + £37.49

b £56.04 + £34.62

c £49.45 + £75.36

d £86.43 – £36.69

e £63.85 – £27.74

f £94.84 – £76.22

2 Look at the picture in the ● activity and answer these questions about the Summer Fair.

a How much did the face painting and coconut shy raise?

b How much did the ice cream and lucky dip raise?

c How much more did the lucky dip raise than the hoopla?

d How much more did the ice cream raise than the face painting?

e The hoopla had been aiming to raise £100. How much less than this did they make?

 These are the amounts raised by all the stalls at the Summer Fair. Use your calculator to work out the answers to these questions.

a   What is the difference between the stall that raised the most and the stall that raised the least?

b   How much did the coconut shy and the hoopla raise together?

c   The face painting and the ice cream stall had hoped to raise £150 together. How much more did they need to have raised?

d   What is the total amount raised?

e   The head teacher added up the totals and arrived at the answer of £335.82. Which stall has she forgotten to include?

f   A local business said it would make the total up to £1000. How much do they need to donate to the school?

 Look at the pictures in the 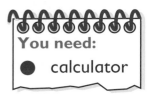 activity. If all the stalls had made 10% more, how much would each of them have made?

Round any decimal numbers with three places you get on your calculator to two decimal places.

What would the new total be?

You need:
● calculator

Proportion

● **Solve problems involving proportions**

Fill in these tables.

a For every £1 Jack saves, his brother Joshua saves £3.
Copy and complete the table showing their savings.

Jack	Joshua
£1	£3

b For every two boys in the class there are three girls.
Copy and complete the table showing the boys and girls in the class.

Boys	Girls
2	3

c At home, for every two cakes that mum eats, dad eats four.
Copy and complete the table showing how many cakes they eat.

Mum	Dad
2	4

1 The sweets I buy always have two orange ones for every four red ones.
Copy and complete the table.

Orange	Red
2	4

a What is the ratio of orange sweets to red ones?

b How many red sweets would I have if I had 12 orange ones?

c How many orange sweets would I have if I had 32 red ones?

2 For every £2 pocket money I get my younger brother gets 50p.
Copy and complete the table showing our pocket money.

Me	My brother
£2	50p

a What is the ratio of my pocket money to my brother's?
b If my brother has £1 how much will I have?
c If we both save our money for eight weeks how much will we each have?

3 The recipe says that I need three eggs for every 10 party cakes.
Copy and complete the table showing the ratio of eggs to cakes.

Eggs	Cakes
3	10

a What is the ratio of eggs to cakes?
b If I want to make 30 cakes how many eggs will I need?
c If I buy a dozen eggs how many cakes can I make?

Answer these word problems.
a I have bought 81 plants. Some are white and some pink. The ratio of pink to white plants is 2 to 7. How many of each colour plant do I have?
b I have 30 tomatoes so I can makes 6 litres of sauce. What is the ratio of tomatoes to sauce?
c I have two cats. One eats twice as much as the other. This week they have eaten 42 tins of food.
How much did each cat eat?

In proportion

Work out the word problems. You may want to copy and complete the table to help you.

a The cat has three spoonfuls of food for every one the kitten has. I dished out 16 spoonfuls of food. How many does the cat have and how many does the kitten have?

Cat	Kitten	Total spoons
3	1	4

b Dad has made 25 cakes for me and him to eat. For each one he gives me, he has four. How many cakes do I get and how many does he get?

Me	Dad	Total cakes
1	4	5

c Every day I eat one apple for every two bananas. This week I have eaten 18 pieces of fruit. How many apples and how many bananas have I eaten?

Apples	Bananas	Total fruit
1	2	3

Work out the problems using the proportions given. Draw a table to help you if you need to.

a Every box of biscuits has four chocolate biscuits for every five digestives. I buy a box of 36 biscuits. How many chocolate and how many digestives will I have?

b There are 63 children going on the school outing. For every three boys going there are four girls. How many boys and how many girls are going?

c In every bag of apples you buy there are three red apples and five green. I buy four bags. How many red and how many green apples will I have?

d In my savings box I have four 10 pences for every six 2 pences. Altogether I have 30 coins. How many 10 pences and how many 2 pences do I have?

e On my necklace I have two round beads for every seven square beads. The necklace has 45 beads altogether. How many square and how many round beads are there?

I have counted all my t-shirts and altogether I have 50. For every two white t-shirts I have three grey ones.

a How many white t-shirts and how many grey t-shirts do I have?

b What fraction of my t-shirts are grey?

c What fraction of my t-shirts are white?

d What percentage of the t-shirts are grey?

e What percentage of the t-shirts are white?

Reviewing written multiplication and division

● **Use efficient written methods to multiply and divide HTU × U, TU × TU, U.t × U and HTU ÷ U**

Work out the answer to each of the following calculations.
Be sure to estimate your answer first.

1
a 653 × 6
b 572 × 7
c 328 × 5
d 725 × 4

e 352 × 9
f 486 × 3
g 832 × 2
h 667 × 7

i 947 × 6
j 768 × 8
k 123 × 5
l 704 × 4

2
a 6·5 × 3
b 4·8 × 7
c 2·8 × 8
d 5·9 × 6

e 6·3 × 4
f 3·7 × 5
g 7·7 × 9
h 9·2 × 6

i 8·6 × 8
j 5·7 × 3
k 8·3 × 4
l 9·6 × 7

Example

678 × 4 → 680 × 4 = 2720

×	600	70	8
4	2400	280	32

```
  2400
   280
 +  32
 ‾‾‾‾‾
  2712
    1
```

or

```
   678
 ×   4
 ‾‾‾‾‾
  2400  (600 × 4)
   280  ( 70 × 4)
    32  (  8 × 4)
 ‾‾‾‾‾
  2712
    1
```

or

```
   678
 ×   4
 ‾‾‾‾‾
  2712
  3 3
```

5·8 × 7 → 6 × 7 = 42

×	5·0	0·8
7	35	5·6

40·6

or

```
   5·8
 ×   7
 ‾‾‾‾‾
    35   (5·0 × 8)
   5·6   (0·8 × 8)
 ‾‾‾‾‾
  40·6
     1
```

Work out the answer to each of the following calculations.
Be sure to estimate your answer first.

a 55 × 82	f 28 × 52	k 74 × 64
b 94 × 46	g 46 × 85	l 68 × 73
c 72 × 53	h 86 × 64	m 58 × 84
d 15 × 75	i 64 × 37	n 82 × 35
e 35 × 91	j 92 × 91	o 93 × 82

Example

$68 \times 34 \rightarrow 70 \times 35 = 2450$

×	60	8
30	1800	240
4	240	32

```
  1800                      68
   240                    × 34
   240        or          2040    (60 × 34)
 +  32                     272    ( 8 × 34)
  2312                    2312
```

Work out the answer to each of the following calculations. Be sure to estimate your answer first.

a 685 ÷ 8	f 483 ÷ 7	k 664 ÷ 6
b 452 ÷ 5	g 319 ÷ 5	l 813 ÷ 4
c 831 ÷ 2	h 947 ÷ 9	m 357 ÷ 8
d 964 ÷ 6	i 557 ÷ 3	n 741 ÷ 7
e 721 ÷ 4	j 264 ÷ 8	o 962 ÷ 9

Example

$645 \div 9 \rightarrow 630 \div 9 = 70$

```
      645         or    9)645        or    9)645   71 R6
    − 630 (70 × 9)     − 630 (70 × 9)        63
      15                15                   15
    −  9 ( 1 × 9)     −  9 ( 1 × 9)        −  9
       6                 6                    6
 Answer = 71 R6      Answer = 71 R6
```

Methods of calculating

● Choose and use appropriate calculation strategies

 1 Look carefully at the numbers in each calculation.
For each pair of cards, decide which calculation is the easiest to work out.
(Do not work out the answers.)

2 Explain your reasons.

a | 26 × 19 | 26 × 91 |

b | 357 ÷ 7 | 456 ÷ 7 |

c | 231 × 9 | 319 × 2 |

d | 66 × 39 | 96 × 63 |

e | 8 × 51 | 8 × 43 |

f | 356 ÷ 2 | 356 ÷ 3 |

g | 480 ÷ 20 | 263 ÷ 9 |

h | 809 ÷ 4 | 609 ÷ 4 |

i | 845 ÷ 5 | 752 ÷ 5 |

j | 49 × 30 | 63 × 30 |

1 Look at the calculations in the ▢ activity.
Find the answers to the five easiest calculations.
Work the answers out in your head.

2 For each of the calculations on page 117 work out the answer in two different ways.
Show clearly your working out each time.

Example

86 × 9

Method 1

86 × 9 = (86 × 10) − 86
    = 860 − 86
    = 774

Method 2

```
              8  6
        ×        9
(80 × 9)  7  2  0
 (6 × 9)        5  4
          7  7  4
```

a 26×19 **b** $623 \div 7$ **c** 25×43

d $495 \div 9$ **e** 234×9 **f** 13×14

g 253×8 **h** 71×22 **i** 56×51

3 Look back at the two different methods you used for each of the calculations in question **2**. For each of the calculations, place a star (☆) beside the method you prefer.

The **6** key on this calculator is missing.
To find out the answer to 36×23

I can do:

$$35 \times 23 = \quad 805$$
$$+ 1 \times 23 = \quad \underline{23}$$
$$\underline{828}$$

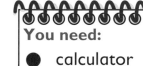

You need:
● calculator

Or I could do:

$$40 \times 23 = \quad 920$$
$$- 4 \times 23 = \quad \underline{92}$$
$$\underline{828}$$

For each of the following calculations, think of two different ways of working out the answers without using the number 6.

a 76×52 **b** 116×33 **c** 264×20

d 68×39 **e** 66×23 **f** 39×666

g 1006×26 **h** 606×35 **i** 996×46

Finding out about odd and even numbers

Explore properties and propose a general statement about numbers

Copy and complete each table by finding numbers that fit.

a Even

×	4		
Even 4	8		
8			
6			

b Odd

×	5	9	
Odd 3			

c Odd

×	7		
Even 2			

Copy and complete these statements. Use the numbers shown to help you.

a The sum of three even numbers is ⬜.

c The product of two even numbers is ⬜.

d The sum of any odd number and any even number is ⬜.

b The difference between two odd numbers is ⬜.

e The difference between two even numbers is ⬜.

55

77

5

36

42

64

3

58

24

118

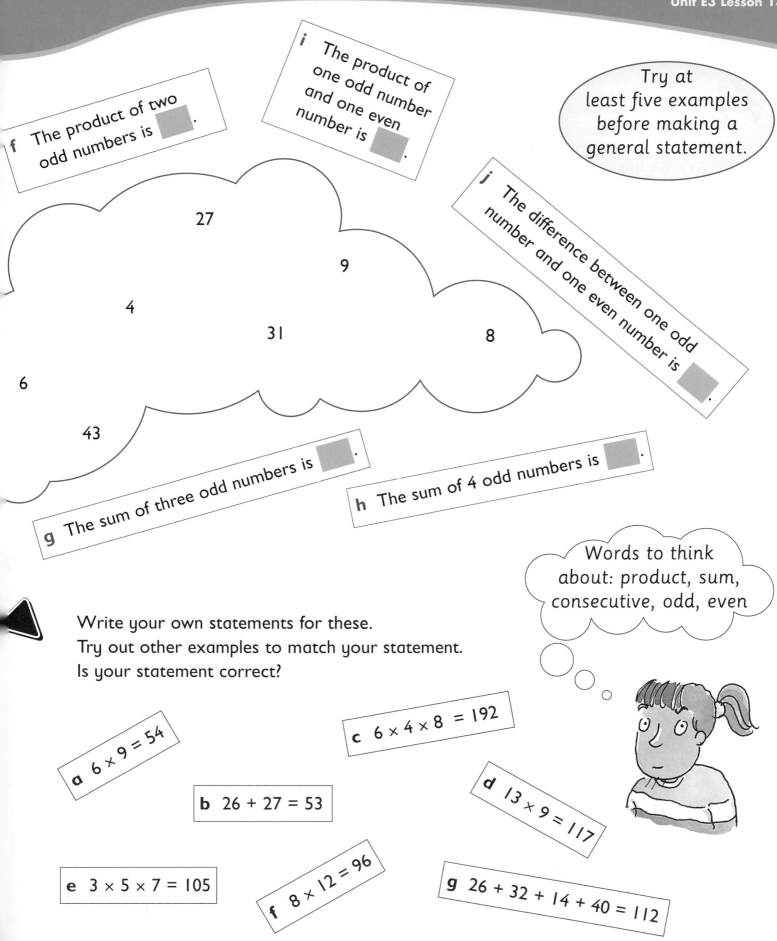

f The product of two odd numbers is ▢.

i The product of one odd number and one even number is ▢.

Try at least five examples before making a general statement.

27

9

4

31

8

6

43

j The difference between one odd number and one even number is ▢.

g The sum of three odd numbers is ▢.

h The sum of 4 odd numbers is ▢.

Words to think about: product, sum, consecutive, odd, even

Write your own statements for these.
Try out other examples to match your statement.
Is your statement correct?

a $6 \times 9 = 54$

c $6 \times 4 \times 8 = 192$

b $26 + 27 = 53$

d $13 \times 9 = 117$

e $3 \times 5 \times 7 = 105$

f $8 \times 12 = 96$

g $26 + 32 + 14 + 40 = 112$

Number sequences

● **Explain a generalised relationship in words**

 Write the next 10 numbers in each of these number sequences using the rule shown.

a The rule is add 3 each time.

336, 339, ☐, ☐, ☐, ☐, ☐, ☐, ☐, ☐, ☐, ☐
+3 +3 +3

b The rule is subtract 5 each time.

625, 620, ☐, ☐, ☐, ☐, ☐, ☐, ☐, ☐, ☐, ☐
−5 −5

c The rule is add 11 each time.

−99, −88, ☐, ☐, ☐, ☐, ☐, ☐, ☐, ☐, ☐
−11 +11

d The rule is halve each time.

10 240, 5120, ☐, ☐, ☐, ☐, ☐, ☐, ☐, ☐, ☐, ☐
÷2 ÷2

e The rule is multiply by 2 each time.

3, 6, ☐, ☐, ☐, ☐, ☐, ☐, ☐, ☐, ☐
×2 ×2

f The rule is add the two previous numbers.

1, 2, 3, 5, ☐, ☐, ☐, ☐, ☐, ☐, ☐, ☐
0 + 1 1 + 2 2 + 3 3 + 4

 1 Identify the rule in each sequence and write it down.
Then write the next five numbers.

Example

87→91→95→99→103→107→111→115

The rule is add 4 each time.

a 514, 520, 526, ☐, ☐, ☐, ☐, ☐

The rule is

b 2, 20, 200, ☐, ☐, ☐, ☐, ☐

The rule is

c 1, 3, 6, 10, ▢, ▢, ▢, ▢, ▢   (The rule is)

d 3, 6, 8, 11, ▢, ▢, ▢, ▢, ▢   (The rule is)

e 2, 4, 6, 10, ▢, ▢, ▢, ▢, ▢   (The rule is)

f 298, 287, 276, ▢, ▢, ▢, ▢, ▢   (The rule is)

g −48, −42, −36, ▢, ▢, ▢, ▢, ▢   (The rule is)

h 4, 40, 20, 200, 100, ▢, ▢, ▢, ▢, ▢   (The rule is)

2 The rule for this number sequence is 'double and subtract 1'.
Write the missing numbers to complete each sequence.

a 2 , 3 , 5 , 9 , ▢   b ▢ , 13, 25, 49

c 12, ▢ , ▢ , 89, 177   d 10, 19, 37, ▢ , ▢

3 The rule is to add the same number each time.
Write the missing numbers to complete the sequences.

a | 2 | | | 18 | b | 10 | | | 58 |

c | 50 | | | 150 | d | 3 | | | 407 |

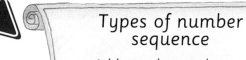

Types of number sequence

– Add or subtract the same number each time.

– Multiply or divide the same number each time.

– Add or subtract a changing number.

– Add the previous two numbers.

– Combine two operations.

1 Write the type of number sequence for each example in question **1** in the ⬤ activity.

2 Construct two number sequences of your own for each type of number sequence shown.

3 Rewrite your sequences on a separate piece of paper, deleting some of the numbers.
Give the sequences to a friend to complete.

You need:
● pencil and paper

Number patterns

● Explain a generalised relationship in words

You need:
● coloured pencils

 1 Look at the pattern below.

a Count the number of dots in each sequence.

b Turn the dot sequence into a number sequence and write the number sequence.

c What is the rule?

2 Look at the pattern below.

a Count the number of dots in each sequence.

b Turn the dot sequence into a number sequence and write the number sequence.

c What is the rule?

 Look at each of the patterns on page 123.

● Draw the next three patterns for each sequence.

● Write an addition number sentence for each.

● Identify and write the rule for extending each sequence.

● Write how many shapes will be in the 10th and 12th pattern.

a

b

c

d

 1 Make your own number patterns.

2 Start with one, two or three shapes.

3 Draw the first four patterns for each sequence.

4 Swap patterns with a friend.

5 Complete the next three patterns of each sequence.

6 Work out the rule for each sequence.

Maths Facts

The seven steps to problem solving

1 Read the problem carefully. **2** What do you have to find?

3 What facts are given? **4** Which of the facts do you need?

5 Make a plan. **6** Carry out your plan to obtain your answer. **7** Check your answer.

Number

Positive and negative numbers

$$-10 \quad -9 \quad -8 \quad -7 \quad -6 \quad -5 \quad -4 \quad -3 \quad -2 \quad -1 \quad 0 \quad 1 \quad 2 \quad 3 \quad 4 \quad 5 \quad 6 \quad 7 \quad 8 \quad 9 \quad 10$$

Place value

1000	2000	3000	4000	5000	6000	7000	8000	9000
100	200	300	400	500	600	700	800	900
10	20	30	40	50	60	70	80	90
1	2	3	4	5	6	7	8	9
0·1	0·2	0·3	0·4	0·5	0·6	0·7	0·8	0·9
0·01	0·02	0·03	0·04	0·05	0·06	0·07	0·08	0·09
0·001	0·002	0·003	0·004	0·005	0·006	0·007	0·008	0·009

Fractions, decimals and percentages

$\frac{1}{100} = 0·01 = 1\%$

$\frac{10}{100} = \frac{1}{10} = 0·1 = 10\%$

$\frac{25}{100} = \frac{1}{4} = 0·25 = 25\%$

$\frac{2}{3} = 0·667 = 66\frac{2}{3}\%$

$\frac{2}{100} = \frac{1}{50} = 0·02 = 2\%$

$\frac{1}{8} = 0·125 = 12·5\%$

$\frac{1}{3} = 0·333 = 33\frac{1}{3}\%$

$\frac{75}{100} = \frac{3}{4} = 0·75 = 75\%$

$\frac{5}{100} = \frac{1}{20} = 0·05 = 5\%$

$\frac{20}{100} = \frac{1}{5} = 0·2 = 20\%$

$\frac{50}{100} = \frac{1}{2} = 0·5 = 50\%$

$\frac{100}{100} = 1 = 100\%$

Number facts

Multiplication and division facts

	×1	×2	×3	×4	×5	×6	×7	×8	×9	×10
×1	1	2	3	4	5	6	7	8	9	10
×2	2	4	6	8	10	12	14	16	18	20
×3	3	6	9	12	15	18	21	24	27	30
×4	4	8	12	16	20	24	28	32	36	40
×5	5	10	15	20	25	30	35	40	45	50
×6	6	12	18	24	30	36	42	48	54	60
×7	7	14	21	28	35	42	49	56	63	70
×8	8	16	24	32	40	48	56	64	72	80
×9	9	18	27	36	45	54	63	72	81	90
×10	10	20	30	40	50	60	70	80	90	100

Tests of divisibility

2 The last digit is 0, 2, 4, 6 or 8.

3 The sum of the digits is divisible by 3.

4 The last two digits are divisible by 4.

5 The last digit is 5 or 0.

6 It is divisible by both 2 and 3.

7 Check a known near multiple of 7.

8 Half of it is divisible by 4 *or*
The last 3 digits are divisible by 8.

9 The sum of the digits is divisible by 9.

10 The last digit is 0.

Calculations

Addition

Whole numbers
Example: 6845 + 5758

```
  6845              6845
+ 5758            + 5758
 11 000            12 603
  1 500             ı ıı
    90
    13
 12 603
   ı
```

Decimals
Example: 26.48 + 5.375

```
  26.48            26.48
+  5.375         +  5.375
 20.000           31.855
 11.000            ı  ı
  0.700
  0.150
  0.005
 31.855
```

Subtraction

Whole numbers
Example: 7845 − 2367

```
  7845      or                 700    ı30    ı5        7 ı3ı5
− 2367                         700    ı40     5         7̶8̶4̶5̶
    33 → 2400      7000 + 800 + 40 + 5                − 2367
  5445 → 7845    − 2000 + 300 + 60 + 7                  5478
  5478             5000 + 400 + 70 + 8
```

Decimals
Example: 639.35 − 214.46

```
  639.35    or                     8 ı2ı5
− 214.46                        6̶3̶9̶.3̶5̶
   00.54 → 215                 − 214.46
  424.35 → 639.35               424.89
  424.89
```

Multiplication

Whole numbers
Example: 5697 × 8

×	8
5000	40000
600	4800
90	720
7	56
	45576

```
  5697                  5697
×    8                ×    8
 40000  (8 × 5000)     45576
  4800  (8 × 600)       5 7 5
   720  (8 × 90)
    56  (8 × 7)
 45576
```

Decimals
Example: 865.56 × 7

×	7
800	5600
60	420
5	35
0.50	3.5
0.06	0.42
	6058.92

```
  865.56                 865.56
×      7               ×      7
  5600   (7 × 800)      6058.92
   420   (7 × 60)        4 3 3 4
    35   (7 × 5)
   3.5   (7 × 0.50)
  0.42   (7 × 0.06)
 6058.92
```

Whole numbers
Example: 364 × 87

×	80	7
300	24000	2100
60	4800	420
4	320	28

26100
5220
348
31668

```
   364
×   87
 24000   (300 × 80)
  4800   (60 × 80)
   320   (4 × 80)
  2100   (300 × 7)
   420   (60 × 7)
    28   (4 × 7)
 31668
   ı ı
```

```
   364
×   87
 29120   364 × 80
  2548   364 × 7
 31668
   ı
```

Calculations

Division

Whole numbers
Example: 337 ÷ 8

```
8) 337
 - 80    (8 × 10)
  257
 - 80    (8 × 10)
  177
 - 80    (8 × 10)
   97
 - 80    (8 × 10)
   17
 - 16    (8 × 2)
    1       42

Answer   42 R 1
```

→

```
8) 337
 - 320   (8 × 40)
   17
 - 16    (8 × 2)
    1       42

Answer   42 R 1
```

→

```
      42   R 1
8) 337
   32
   17
   16
    1
```

→

```
      42   R 1
8) 337
```

Decimals

Example: 78.3 ÷ 9

```
9) 78.3
 - 72.0   (9 × 8)
    6.3
 -  6.3   (9 × 0.7)
      0      8.7

Answer   8.7
```

Example: 48.6 ÷ 3

```
3) 48.6
 - 30.0   (3 × 10)
   18.6
 - 18.0   (3 × 6)
    0.6
 -  0.6   (3 × 0.2)
      0      16.2

Answer   16.2
```

Order of operations

Brackets → Division → Multiplication → Addition → Subtraction

Shape and space

2–D shapes

 circle

 semi-circle

 right-angled triangle

 equilateral triangle

 isosceles triangle

 scalene triangle

 square

 rectangle

 rhombus

 kite

 parallelogram

 trapezium

 pentagon

 hexagon

 heptagon

 octagon

Shape and space

3–D solids

 cube

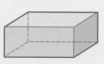 cuboid

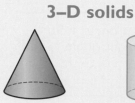 cone

 cylinder

 sphere

 hemi-sphere

 triangular prism

 triangular-based pyramid (tetrahedron)

 square-based pyramid

 octahedron

 dodecahedron

Co-ordinates

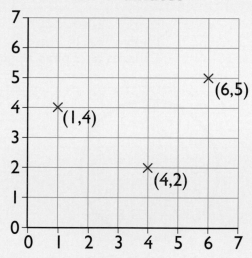

Reflection

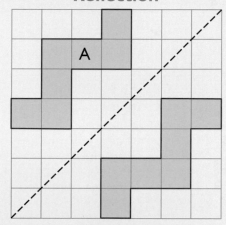

Shape A has been reflected along the diagonal line of symmetry

Rotation

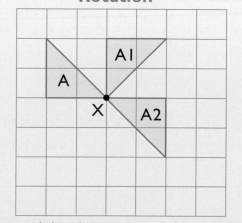

Shape A has been rotated through 90° (Shape A1) and 180° (Shape A2) around Point X

Translation

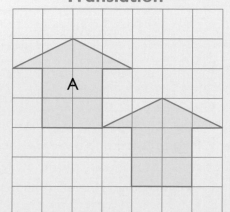

Shape A has been translated 3 squares to the right and 2 squares down.

Shape and space

Angles

Acute angle < 90°
Obtuse angle > 90° and < 180°
Reflex angle > 180° and < 360°
4 right angles (complete turn) = 360°

Right angle = 90°
Straight angle = 180°

Lines

Parallel lines

Perpendicular lines

Measures

Length

1 km	=	1000 m	=	100 000 cm		
0·1 km	=	100 m	=	10 000 cm	=	100 000 mm
0·01 km	=	10 m	=	1000 cm	=	10 000 mm
1 m	=	100 cm	=	1000 mm		
0·1 m	=	10 cm	=	100 mm		
0·01 m	=	1 cm	=	10 mm		
1 cm	=	10 mm		0·1 cm	=	1 mm

Mass

1 t	=	1000 kg	1 kg	=	1000 g
0.1 kg	=	100 g	0.01 kg	=	10 g

Capacity

1 litre	=	1000 ml	0.1 l	=	100 ml
0.01 l	=	10 ml	1 cl	=	10 ml

Metric units and imperial units

Length
8 km ≈ 5 miles (1 mile ≈ 1.6 km)

Mass
1 kg ≈ 2.2 lb
30 g ≈ 1 oz

Capacity
1 litre ≈ $1\frac{3}{4}$ pints
4.5 litres ≈ 8 pints (1 gallon)

Time

1 millennium	=	1000 years
1 century	=	100 years
1 decade	=	10 years
1 year	=	12 months
	=	365 days
	=	366 days (leap year)
1 week (wk)	=	7 days
1 day	=	24 hours
1 minute (min)	=	60 seconds

24 hour time

Perimeter and Area

P = perimeter   A = area   l = length   b = breadth

Perimeter of a rectangle:
P = 2l + 2b   or   P = 2 x (l + b)

Perimeter of a square:
P = 4 x l

Area of a rectangle:
A = l x b

Handling data

Planning an investigation

1 Describe your investigation.   **2** Do you have a prediction?   **3** Describe the data you need to collect.
4 How will you record and organise the data?   **5** What diagrams will you use to illustrate the data?
6 What statistics will you calculate?   **7** How will you analyse the data and come to a conclusion?
8 When you have finished, describe how your investigation could be improved.

Mode
The value that occurs most often.

Range
Difference between the largest value and the smallest value.

Median
Middle value when all the values have been ordered smallest to largest.

Mean
Total of all the values divided by the number of values.